Illuminated Manuscripts

Illuminated Manuscripts

JANICE ANDERSON

TODTRI

This book was designed and produced by TODTRI Book Publishers
P.O. Box 572, New York, NY 10116-0572
Fax: (212) 695-6984
e-mail: todtri@mindspring.com

Printed and bound in Singapore

ISBN 1-57717-155-1

Visit us on the web!
www.todtri.com

Author: Janice Anderson

Publisher: Robert M. Tod
Editor: Nicolas Wright
Art Director: Ron Pickless
Typesetting & DTP: Blanc Verso UK

CONTENTS

INTRODUCTION 7

MAKING ILLUMINATED MANUSCRIPTS 15

EARLY MEDIEVAL EUROPE 37

CELTIC IRELAND AND ENGLAND 59

A GOLDEN AGE ~ 1150–1350 81

PATRONAGE AND THE MANUSCRIPT 95

THE RENAISSANCE AND AFTER 111

INDEX 126

INTRODUCTION

Some of the most glorious works of art created during the Middle Ages were in book – or, to give it the correct style of the period, codex – form. They were made for those very highly decorated codices which we call 'illuminated manuscripts', the word 'illuminated' coming from the Latin word illuminare, meaning 'adorned'.

Before the age of printing, everything that went into the making of a book, beginning with making the papyrus or preparing the animal skin on which it was written, then inscribing the text, decorating or illustrating it, gathering it into folios (pages), making a cover for it and binding it all together, was done by hand.

Making the simplest book, one which contained just hand-written text, was a slow and painstaking procedure. Even so, hundreds of thousands of books were created in the twelve centuries or so between the time the codex replaced the roll as the accepted shape for a book and the invention of printing from movable type in the mid-fifteenth century.

A very small number of these books – five per cent is a recent estimation – were considered important enough to be made beautiful by the addition of decoration and pictorial embellishment, much of it involving the use of the precious metals gold and silver which added greatly to their glowing, jewel-like beauty.

THE ORIGINS OF MANUSCRIPT ILLUMINATION

It has been said that without the codex to propagate its message, Christianity would never have become more than a minor Middle Eastern sect. And in an age when most people, even great rulers, were illiterate, illustration and decorating assumed an enormous importance, because they told the Bible stories in a way most people could understand and made the Christian message interesting and exciting.

Since very few early codices have survived, it is hard to set a date for when manuscripts first began to be decorated and illustrated. It is likely to have been early on, since we know that the desire to beautify texts is a very old one. Ancient Egyptian scrolls containing splendidly coloured drawings, including some with gold embellishments, are known, as are illustrated versions of *The Book of the Dead*, which it was customary to bury with a dead

Above: A large antiphonal in Latin from the Circle of Pellegrino Di Mariano, *c.* 1480.

Opposite: A classic example of one of the earliest forms of illuminated manuscripts, the *Book of the Dead*, created by the ancient Egyptians. It was customary to bury such manuscripts with a dead person, to help their soul pass into the afterlife.

Above: A gory depiction of the massacre of rebellious French peasants in 1358 by the Dauphin's troops at Neux. This is from the Froissart Manuscripts.

person to help his soul pass through the nether world.

Another pointer to an early date for illustration being included in codices is the fact that among the few very early codices still surviving in European libraries are several illustrated ones dating from the fifth century AD. The Vatican Library in Rome has two versions of the works of Virgil each of which contains splendid illustrations, in markedly different but equally confident styles, suggesting that the artists were working with an art no longer in its infancy.

It is no accident that illuminated manuscripts reflect the other arts of the periods in which they were written, from architecture to ivory carving, wood and stone carving to jewellery making, enamelling and mosaics. Even the local styles of such minor arts as weaving, needlework and embroidery could be picked up by painters and illuminators and used in the decorating of manuscripts.

The ways these minor arts were designed and practised would

naturally be followed by local painters and illuminators in their own work. Thus the metalwork designs and stone and wood carving of the Celts in Ireland were used to stunning effect in many great manuscripts and, centuries later, illuminators of manuscripts were taking the styles of wall paintings and mosaics in early Romanesque churches and the stained glass pictures in the windows of Gothic churches and putting them into their manuscripts.

It was a double bonus for books, for not only were the artists of the illuminated book regularly finding fresh ideas and new styles for their work, but they were making pictures whose style would be recognizable and comfortably familiar to everyone who worshipped in church.

CATEGORIES OF ILLUMINATED BOOKS

In the early Middle Ages, when most manuscript illumination was the work of monks and nuns, most of the books produced were religious and intended for use in churches and monasteries. Apart from such important texts as St Augustine's *The City of God* or St Benedict's *Rule*, and the writings of the heads of important monastic

Above: A fifteenth-century monk poring over his work, copying a manuscript. This is a Grisaille form the manuscript Miracles de Notre Dame, reproduced in *Les Arts Somptuaires*, volume two.

schools – Alcuin at Tours or St Ethelwold at Winchester, for instance – there was very little new writing in the Middle Ages, so that most work was copying Biblical texts.

The biggest category of religious books involved the reproduction of the text of the Bible, including the whole Bible in one volume, individual books of the Old Testament, collections of the 150 psalms (psalters), and collections of the first four books of the New Testament (gospels).

Bibles produced in the early Middle Ages were usually very large and intended to be set on lecterns for reading in churches and monasteries. From about the thirteenth century, smaller, one-volume Bibles were produced in large numbers, for use by students, for private devotions and for carrying by itinerant friars, who used them for preaching and teaching.

Psalters had a particular significance in that they were the religious books most used by lay people in the early Middle Ages, both at home for private devotions and in church. Of course, one had to be fairly well off to afford them, so they became something of a status symbol and, if specially commissioned, might include in their lists of saints' days ones of particular significance to their owner, as well as prayers and other texts asked for by the owner.

Later in the Middle Ages, when more people could read and the Church had become more relaxed about personal devotion outside the religious buildings, the psalter was superseded by the book of hours, an example of which had to be in every royal, noble, or just plain rich household. Books of hours were used to recite prayers from at prescribed times of day – known as the liturgical hours. Some of the most celebrated of all illuminated manuscripts were books of hours, produced in the fifteenth century.

Liturgical books, necessary for the celebration of church services, made up the second largest category of religious books. These would include psalters and gospels again, sacramentaries, lectionaries and pericopes (collections of extracts for reading in church).

Later in the Middle Ages, these separate service books were assembled together into volumes called missals. Their embellishment, which was concerned with emphasizing the different elements of the service,

Above: Christ presents the Mission to St. Peter, following the Gospel of St. Mathew, when Christ says 'Thou art Peter and upon this rock I will build my Church'. Artist: Joahannes Von Valkenburg.

Opposite: The flight into Egypt with a young Joseph leading the donkey on which the Virgin and child are seated. This is from a French *Book of Hours* on vellum *c*.1450.

Previous pages: A beautiful extract from a *Book of Hours*, showing a visitation by the Madonna. Created in Poitiers *c*.1460.

concentrated very much on initials and the use of red lettering.

Into a third category of religious book fell those books which were extra to Christian worship, and included apocalypses (copies of the last book of the New Testament, the Book of Revelations), lives of the saints, and graduals (the main choir book used during Masses) and antiphonals (containing sung parts of the Divine Office).

While a few secular manuscripts, such as astronomical treatises and copies of classical writers were produced from early on, the spread of knowledge, accompanied by the founding of universities throughout Europe in the later Middle Ages, led to a great increase in the production of secular texts. Among those chosen most often for the full illuminated manuscript treatment were histories and chronicles; reproductions of the works of the great classical writers such as the Greek philosophers Plato and Aristotle, and the Roman writers Virgil, Ovid and Horace; bestiaries, which were more than simple descriptions of animals and birds for they also contained myths, legends and tales with a moral or symbolic meaning; herbals; and romances and other literature.

MAKING
ILLUMINATED
MANUSCRIPTS

A book, in its broadest sense, is a manuscript written so that others may know, and perhaps learn from or be entertained by, what the writer has to say. The ancient Egyptians produced manuscripts 3,000 years before the birth of Christ. They were in the form of rolls (*or rotuli*) — long strips of papyrus rolled up by the short edges.

Papyrus, made from the stems of a plant, also called papyrus, which grew along the marshy edges of the Nile, was used by the Egyptians from about 3000BC and remained the main material for writing and drawing on in Classical Greece and throughout the Roman Empire. It was still in use in Europe for everyday writings such as letters and accounts until well into the tenth century and beyond: papyrus was used as a writing material in the Vatican Library until the later Middle Ages. Although it was a rather limp material, papyrus sheets were sometimes gathered together into codex form, with leaves of vellum added to the gatherings to give them some stiffness.

Pliny the Elder wrote in his *Natural History* that animal skin, or parchment, came into general use after the Ptolemaic kings who ruled Egypt for three centuries after the death of Alexander the Great, forbade the export of papyrus from Egypt in the second century BC in a vain attempt to prevent Eumenes II of Pergamon, a Hellenistic settlement in Turkey, building up his great library. Eumenes, like Alexandra the

Above: The Emperor Constantine realised the importance of books in propagating the Christian message and established many scriptoria in his great new city, Constantinople.

Opposite: Eadwine, a Benedictine monk at Canterbury in the twelfth century, inscribes a manuscript, holding both a quill and a knife for sharpening it. Eadwine Psalter, England, *c*.1150.

rerum furdarum ac fenf

Great before him at Alexandria, and Constantine the Great at Constantinople after him, was intent on turning his city into a great centre of learning. With papyrus unavailable to him, Eumenes simply turned to the animal skins which Herodutus had noted being used in the region centuries before. Animal skins, carefully cleaned and stretched, could be made into parchment, both sides of which could be used for writing on. Parchment turned out to be not just a substitute for papyrus but something infinitely better; it was less liable to deterioration and its shape — most skins were roughly rectangular — made it easier to handle.

HOW THE SCROLL BECAME THE BOOK

The change from the rolled-up scroll of the Ancient World to the kind of book we know today — many leaves of the writing material bound together between heavier covers — occurred gradually during the first to the fifth centuries AD. The first book-shaped form, called a codex, developed naturally from the wax-covered writing tablets or boards, carried several at a time and held together by rings pushed through holes at their edges, which were used throughout the Roman world for making notes, inventories or lists or simply for jotting down ideas, doing sums, and so on. Marks on the waxed surface could be smoothed out and the tablets used again.

The codex form was soon found to be much more serviceable than papyrus scrolls. There was more space available for writing and for adding decoration around the text or including illustrations relevant to the text. A text that needed 30 or 40 feet of papyrus roll to accommodate it could be fitted comfortably into a codex with 40 or 50 leaves (and therefore with 80 or 100 pages, or folios). Thus, the codex was easier to handle than the roll and also easier to store.

Sheep and calves provided the best skins for parchment, though the skins of oxen, goats, pigs and asses were all useful, if not for fine parchment, then for heavier covers and bindings

Left: Gathering gourds: an illustration from a Renaissance edition of the Roman writer Pliny the Elder's *Historia Naturalis*, made at Siena in Italy.

Overleaf: A surgeon at work: from Pliny the Elder's *Historia Naturalis*, Italy.

ENSI
homin
euo pri
non ital
etiam i
pe euro
quoque
nec per
lias ue
magno
alibi q̄
sine do
ac sine
sed tan
quæeau
renda

qui non abijt in consilio
impiorum: & in uia pecca
tor non stetit: & in cathe
dra pestilencie non sedit.

no: domine deus meus magnifi
catus es uehementer.
Confessionem ⁊ decorem induisti:
amictus lumine sicut uestimento.
Extendens celum sicut pellem:
qui tegis aquis superiora eius.
Qui ponis nubem ascensum tuū:
qui ambulas super pennas uen
torum
Qui facis angelos tuos spiritus:
⁊ ministros tuos ignem urentem.
Qui fundasti terram super stabi
litatem suam: non inclinabitur
in seculum seculi.

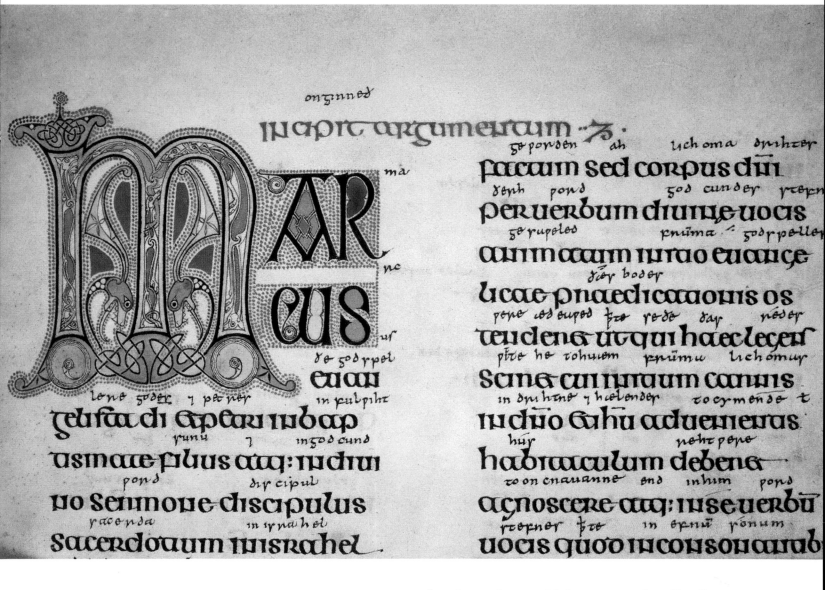

Above: St Mark's portrait page, from the Lindisfarne Gospels. This master-piece of Celtic Saxon (Insular) art was made in honour of St Cuthbert at Lindisfarne in Northumbria, *c.*698.

Opposite: The soul of a dead person descending into the Underworld for judgment: a scene from a *Book of the Dead*, made on papyrus in Ancient Egypt.

Previous pages left: A conventional way of identifying the Biblical King David in manuscripts was to portray him playing a harp. Historiated initial 'B', Peterborough Psalter, England, *c.*1310-20.

Previous pages right: Detail from the Luttrell Psalter, made for Sir Geoffrey Luttrell of Irnham in Lincolnshire. The grotesque (at the foot of the page) — a monster composed of animal and human parts — is typical of the exquisite and imaginative marginal and border decoration of the psalter. England, c.1340.

or for volumes that were likely to receive a lot of handling, such as account books. For the very finest codices, vellum was the first choice for the material on which it was written. This was a particularly fine, sometimes almost transparent, materi-al made from the skins of very young calves or, in the case of 'uterine vellum', from the skins of unborn calves.

MAKING BOOKS

Since Christianity provided the main subjects for codices in early medieval Europe, it is not surprising that the Christian church and its monasteries and other religious houses should also be the main makers of codices during the early medieval period, from about the ninth century to the early thirteenth century.

While most religious houses of any note at all had their writing rooms, a great monastery would have its own scripto-rium, where manuscripts were written and illuminated, and even its own 'parcheminerie', where the parchment and vel-

lum for their books were made. The great Abbey of Cluny, in France, founded as a simple Benedictine monastery in 910, had by the twelfth century become the mother house for a network of some 1,450 dependent priories stretching across Europe and into Britain. By this time, too, Cluny had become celebrated throughout Europe for the quality of the parchment and vellum made there, as well as for the magnificent manuscripts, many of them destined for its daughter churches and monasteries, which came out of its scriptorium.

These manuscripts would be the result of the labours of many people, for no one person could do it all. Making a book by hand was a complicated business. First, the animal skin needed many stages of preparation, involving washing, rinsing, scraping off the hair, and stretching it on frames. Once stretched and dried, it would be scraped again, rubbed with chalk and then rolled up ready for use. When the parchment arrived, suitably prepared, on a monk's desk in the scriptorium, he might choose to rub it smooth again, with pumice; if he did not he might find himself having to work with a sheet of parchment so hairy that his quill and ink did not work easily on it: 'This parchment is certainly hairy,' at least one exasperated scribe is known to have scribbled on his work.

Turning rectangles of parchment into collections of 'sheets' for books involved folding them — in half (bifolios) for large books, twice (quarto size), or three times (octavo size). Several foldings of sheets would then be gathered together, to make gatherings or quires. The binding of several gatherings together between heavy boards or coverings to make the book came later, after the text and decoration was complete.

Design and layout of the pages, as well as their size, depended on the nature of the book being produced. A book intended for quiet study could be smaller and designed with more closely-packed texts than one intended for reading out loud — from a lectern at mealtimes in a monastery refectory or during a service in church, for instance. The design decided

Opposite: A contemporary study of the French-born historian, Jean Froissart, at work. An ilustration from a version of Froissart's *Chronicles, c.*1400.

Overleaf: Hours of the Virgin use of Paris in latin, with calendar in French, made for Catherine of Valois, Queen of England. This scene shows the Annunciation. Artist unknown 1420–1422.

on, including the number of columns of text to go on each page, the pages would be laid out accordingly, perhaps following the advice given in one of the numerous instruction books available for the guidance of manuscript producers. These could be very detailed, even down to giving directions on the size of the space between rules, which itself would depend on the size and style of lettering being used. To ensure that every page was ruled the same, pricks would be made through every folio of a gathering and the pricks on each page joined up by rules, made by fine metal points, that would guide the scribe's pen. Since these rules were often made with coloured pigments, they can still be seen on many manuscripts.

THE WORK OF THE SCRIBE

A scribe would work on a manuscript before an illuminator, whose task was to decorate and illustrate the completed text. The scribe might do the initial pricking and ruling of the parchment sheets himself, or, if he worked in a large monastery scriptorium where some monks were assigned solely to the pricking and ruling, he would start work at once on prepared sheets.

Scribes were copiers rather than writers, for most books produced in the early Middle Ages were copies of earlier texts, including texts from the Ancient Greeks and Romans. Using a goose- or swan-feather quill, which needed sharpening many times during the course of a day's work, and ink, for which there were several recipes, the scribe would carefully copy the text in front of him (or her, for there were women scribes, particularly in nunneries), leaving spaces for initials, miniatures and other elements which might be wanted for important books.

The codex being copied was usually set on a lectern above the scribe's desk. It might have a blank sheet with a hole cut out of it set over the page, so that the scribe would see only one line at a time, thus reducing the chance of his eye jumping a line and his miscopying the precious manuscript. If the text was a relatively simple manuscript, of which several copies were wanted, a number of copyists might sit together and have the work dictated to them.

It was laborious and, especially in winter, when the scribe's fingers and thumbs could ache with cold, painful work. Occasionally, scribes scribbled little notes in the margins of their work, recording their woes, such as 'Thank God it will soon be dark', or 'Oh, that I had a good glass of wine'. More often, a scribe, before putting down his quill for the last

Domine
labia
mea a
pies.
t os meum an
nunciabit laudem tuam.
Deus in adiu
torium meum
intende. Domine ad
adiuvandum me
festina. Gloria pa
tri filio et spiritui sancto.
Sicut erat in princi

Comment le duc de lancastir et le duc de
bresuy vindrent a paris pour eulz cõbat
renant le roy. mais le roy prist le fait

en la main...

...ans ceus cinqãte deux
la veille de la nie dame
...mi aoust. se combati
...mon seigneur Guy de
...colle Seigneur dau...
...bmõt lors mareschal de france en Bre
taigne. et fu le dit mareschal occis en la

dicte bataille. le Sire de Briquebec le chā
tellain de Beauuais a plusieurs autres no
bles tant du dit pays de bretaigne côme
dautres marches du royaume de france

Item en icelui an. CCCLV. le mardy
quart iour de decembre se dot combatre a
paris un duc dalemaigne appelle le duc de
bresuy contre le duc de lancastre pour pa
roles que le dit duc de lancastre deuoir a
uoir dites du dit duc de bresuy dont il lap
pella en la court du roy de france. Et uin

time on a manuscript, would at the end of it thank the person for whom the work had been done (and who, probably, had also put up the money for it), asking Christ 'to recompense him for ever', or ask for blessings on his own labours: 'May the mother of honour bless the writer's right hand'. Sometimes a scribe's last words on a manuscript would be much more down to earth, such as 'It is finished. Let it be finished and let the writer go out for a drink'.

Of course, by the later Middle Ages and in the Renaissance period, when the making of books had become an occupation and, indeed, a business for people outside the church, many lay men and women worked as scribes, so that the sometimes distinctly worldly tone of their comments on manuscripts – 'Let a pretty girl be given to the writer for his pains', for instance – becomes less shocking if one can assume that it was not written by a monk in holy orders. The last comment sounds as if it might have come from the quill of a student, working to augment his income, a practice not uncommon among students, law clerks, priests, and even educated shopkeepers from about the twelfth and thirteenth centuries on.

While many of the best-known scribes of the early medieval period worked in monasteries – the renowned Benedictine monk, Eadwine, worked at Canterbury in the twelfth century, and Matthew Paris, who was both writer and artist, was at St Albans Abbey in the thirteenth century – there were other places where scribes might be employed. The great patrons of book production, from Charlemagne and the Ottonian emperors down to the great Renaissance patrons of the fifteenth century, employed scribes in their own households as well as commissioning work from monastic scriptoria or lay outsiders. By Renaissance time, too, independent ateliers of illuminators could be found in many great cities – Florence, in Italy, had several in the fifteenth century.

THE SCRIPTS

All the letters used in illuminated manuscripts (and still used in our alphabet today, of course) derived from the Roman alphabet. There were many changes in the style and shape of the letters over the centuries, which can guide scholars in

their efforts to date manuscripts and even to say where they may have been written.

The earliest script used in manuscripts was the uncial form, whose large, rounded letters, with a slight backwards inclination, harking back to the manuscripts of the Romans, first appear in the early centuries AD. Majuscule (large) uncials or half uncials were the letters used in the eighth-century *Lindisfarne Gospels*. Various uncial styles were used in Europe, such as Lombardic, the main hand of Italy and based on the old Roman cursive script; Visigothic, used throughout Spain; Merovingian, the looped, angled and rather cramped hand used in France; and Celtic, a bold and clear hand derived from Roman-style manuscripts taken to Ireland by missionaries.

The century following the period of the *Lindisfarne Gospels* saw the most dramatic change in script style, brought about by Charlemagne's determined revival of learning in Europe. He issued orders that reading and writing must be taught in all the religious houses in his widespread kingdom, telling the great scholar Alcuin of York that 'It was the wisest of men who discovered these arts concerning the nature of things, and it would be a disgrace to let them perish in our day'.

A new style of handwriting, the clear and beautiful Caroline minuscule, was developed and became the style for scribes throughout Charlemagne's empire. It was used, almost without any change in style, from about 850 to 1000, in monasteries to copy not only Bibles, the Gospels, sacramentaries and liturgical calendars, but also to copy the works of many classical writers. Once the eleventh century was under way, the script style changed quite quickly to a lettering that, while still regular and clear, was quite different from Caroline miniscule. It also involved the use of contractions – partly to save parchment and partly because more lay people were learning to write – which are not always clear and easy to read.

During the thirteenth century, when the Gothic style was at its height in European art and architecture, a very decorative style of script, with angular letters, developed from the script currently in use in Europe. This Gothic script was the standard in Europe until the Renaissance, when scholars, influenced by the new Humanist need for clarity and simplicity, rejected the Gothic style in favour of what they thought was the classical Roman script but which was, in fact, the Caroline minuscule in which so many classical texts had been saved from being lost forever in the monastic scriptoria of the Carolingian empire.

This new manuscript style, called Roman, had largely replaced Gothic as a general script by the mid-fifteenth century, just in time to be the script on which a great many printed typefaces were based. Not that Gothic script disappeared, because it remained in use for some time, particularly for religious texts, and numerous printed typefaces were based on it, including the one used to print the famous Gutenberg Bible.

DECORATING AND ILLUSTRATING MANUSCRIPTS

Because the great library at Alexandria was wrecked twice over, burnt first by Julius Caesar and then finally destroyed by the Arabs in the sixth century AD, who are said to have burnt enough books from it 'to heat the baths of the city for six months', we cannot tell how far the Greeks and Romans went in illustrating their manuscripts.

Thus, any history of book illustration in Europe has to start with the advent of the codex, from the first to the fifth centuries AD. During these centuries, the Roman Empire diminished in strength and finally collapsed, while Christianity grew in strength and became the religion of Europe. The codex played a major – some would say an essential – role in propagating Christian beliefs and values, and decorating particularly valuable codices seems to have become an important task early on in its history. Very few original illustrated codices survive from the last centuries of the Roman Empire, though copies of others exist, made in Byzantium and in Carolingian times, but they are enough to give us the impression of the beginnings of a tradition for beautifying books with decoration and illustration.

By the sixth century AD, the elements for illuminating manuscripts were largely in place. By now, codices were being produced containing all the main decorative elements of the illuminated manuscript: initial letters, which could either be elaborately decorated, contain scenes from familiar stories (in which case they are called 'historiated' initials), or contain figures, either human, animal or fantasy ('inhabited' initials); miniatures; borders, which could be either illustrative or decorative; and *bas de page* decorations. Decorative flourishes to fill text lines or finish off decorations were also in evidence. Gold was also being used extensively in codices from the Byzantine school, centred on Constantinople, the great city established on the foundations of Byzantium by Constantine the Great in the fourth century.

The word 'illumination' comes from Latin, in which the word for light is *lumen*, and *illuminare*, when used with oratory, means to adorn with flourishes, and refers to the art of lighting up the pages of a book with bright colours and burnished gold. Although the word 'illuminator' does not seem to have been applied to artists until about the twelfth century, artists were certainly illuminators for several centuries before this, using gold in both leaf and paint form in close harmony with brightly coloured paints on manuscripts. It is true, though, that it was not until the twelfth century that artists perfected the business of layering gold leaf on vellum and then burnishing it so that it glows almost as brightly today as it did when it was first added.

ARTISTS' COLOURS

A wide range of colours was available to the artist, made from minerals ground to a powder and from organic matter, including clays and plants.

Red, especially crimson and vermilion, was the most widely used colour. The tradition for using red on manuscripts began with the Romans, whose ordinances or laws were called rubrics (Latin: *rubrica*, meaning 'red ochre' or 'vermilion') because they were written in vermilion. The practice was carried over into the Christian church, with liturgical books having special directions, rules and orders for services written in red so that they stood out from the rest of the text. It was also the practice from early on in undecorated, text-only manuscripts such as psalters and gospels to colour red the initial letters of psalms and other sections or paragraphs. It is not too much of an exaggeration to say that the whole art of illumination grew out of the desire to decorate these red initials.

Like red, which came in many shades from different minerals and plants – the Roman poet Ovid refers to the crimson juice of whortleberries being used to colour letters on a manuscript – blue, the second most widely used colour on manu-

Opposite: An ornately decorated initial to St Matthew's Gospel, from the Lindisfarne Gospels. By producing such extraordinarily complex and detailed work, the Gospel's illuminator, Monk Eadfrith, Bishop of Lindisfarne, was praising and glorifying God to the limits of his skill.

Overleaf: Book of Hours in latin, use of Rome, with miniatures by the Prayer Book Master. Bruges *c.*1500

onginneð   godspeller

boc

Incipit euangelii

genelogia matthei

LIBER

GENERA

TIONIS

XPI FILII DAVID FILII ABRAHAM

cynn neoce nisse

cneu nisse

ihaelend þe cnyrtes

dauides sunu

abraham þy sunu

...us dai...
...ns in
adiuto
ni me
um in
tende
Domine ad adiuuan
dum me festina Glo
na patri. Hympnus
Memento salnti
anctor quat
nii quondam corpo
ris extlibata uirgie

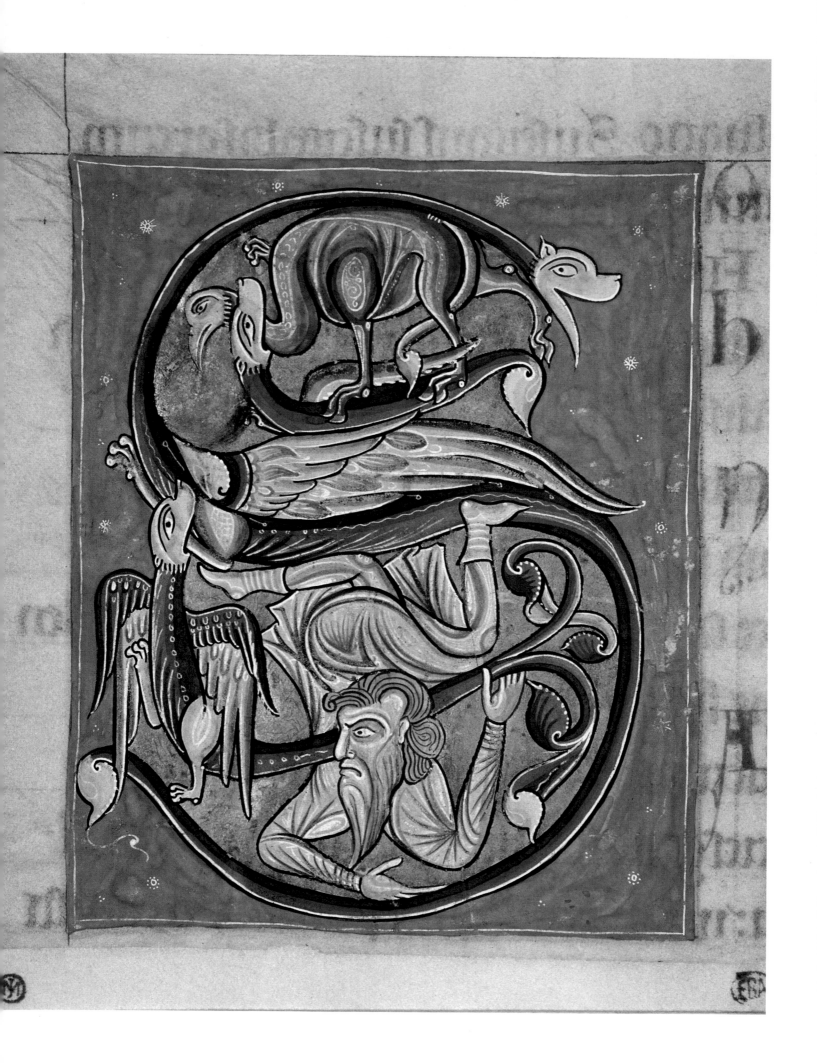

scripts, was also available to the artist in numerous shades from plants and minerals, though minerals supplied the best colours. Azurite, a copper carbonate, was ground to a powder for a good, bright blue; but the most sought-after blue was ultramarine, made from the heavenly blue lapis lazuli, a stone found in Afghanistan. Its rarity made it very expensive, so it was kept for particularly significant areas, such as the robes of the Virgin Mary, on the most beautiful manuscripts.

Greens also came from a mineral, malachite, or from a man-made version of the patina called verdigris which forms naturally on copper, brass or bronze, or from the earth pigment called terre verte. Saffron, a particularly expensive plant, gave artists their best yellow, and white was made from lead oxide.

Colours were usually dissolved in water and mixed with a tempera medium, such as egg white or gum. The point at which an artist began using his paints was dictated by the type of gold also being used on the manuscript. If it was gold leaf, it would be applied to the parchment before any colours; gold paint would be held back till the colours were in place.

Above: A Beatus initial, introducing the 1st Psalm, from the Winchester Bible. The artists have depicted twin themes: David rescuing a lamb from his flock from the jaws of a lion, and Jesus delivering one of his own flock from an evil spirit. Winchester, England, *c.*1150-1180.

GUIDES TO DECORATING

Before using colours, the artist would first draw on to his parchment an outline under-design, with pen and ink, graphite, or perhaps a hard point. The outline was not usually very detailed, since it was intended as an artist's rough only. Like the scribe, the artist had various guides to hand, including exempla and pattern books of birds, animals, plants and human figures, and model books containing ideas for initial letters and borders.

Another guide, which artists knew better than to stray from, was conventional Christian iconography which dictated that certain subjects, and there were many of them, should always be portrayed in the same way, partly to make them readily identifiable – King David playing a harp, for instance, the Virgin Mary with an open devotional book in any depiction of the Annunciation, St Sebastian with his body pierced

with arrows, St Catherine with the wheel on which she was martyred, and many others.

The artistic conventions of the period in which the artist was working also influenced the style of his work. Thus in the thirteenth century, when the Gothic style spread through European art and architecture, it soon began to show in illuminated manuscripts. Borders changed shape so that they mirrored the pointed windows and arches of Gothic churches and miniatures were painted in the colours and shapes of stained glass windows.

This still left artists with plenty of scope for doing their own thing, particularly at the foot of a page, below the text, where many artists, freed from the restraints which hedged about miniatures and initials, either let their imaginations run riot, producing an array of extraordinarily fantastical or grotesque creatures, playful animals or acrobats, dancers and musicians, which by the fourteenth century had come to be known as 'drolleries', or choosing to shows scenes of everyday life from the world around them, thus giving future historians wonderful glimpses of what life was like for ordinary people in medieval times.

Opposite: Imaginery animals and acrobats adorn an initial letter 'S'. Bible of Saint Andrew of the Woods.

EARLY MEDIEVAL EUROPE

Two events, nearly five centuries apart, which had great significance for the history of Europe, also had major effects on the development of the arts, architecture and intellectual life of the Continent and the British Isles.

First, came the Emperor Constantine's founding of the city of Constantinople on what was left of the old Hellenistic and Roman city of Byzantium in the Eastern Roman Empire, around AD 330. Second, on

Above: A 16th-century study of the holy Roman Emperor, Charlemage. Many of the finest illuminated manuscripts of the early medieval period were made at court schools established by him.

Opposite: Numerous versions of Pope Gregory the Great's Registrum Gregorii were made in early medieval Europe.

Christmas Day 800, Charles, King of the Franks, better known to us as Charlemagne, was crowned Emperor by Pope Leo III in Rome. Both these great rulers believed in the importance of learning, of being able to read and write and to know about the past, as the cement which held society – and whole empires – together. Both believed that learning should be based on Christianity. And both saw the book as the main propagator of knowledge, setting up schools and scriptoria devoted to their production.

Although he was a pagan at the time of Constantinople's building, Constantine – who was baptized shortly before his death – saw the Christian church as a major unifying force. Thus, almost from the beginning of their production, codices were associated with Christianity and with the propagation of Christian beliefs and writings: Constantine is known to have ordered the making of 50 copies of the Scriptures, one for each of the churches in his new city.

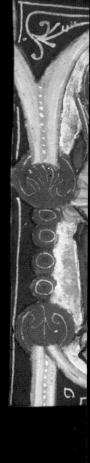

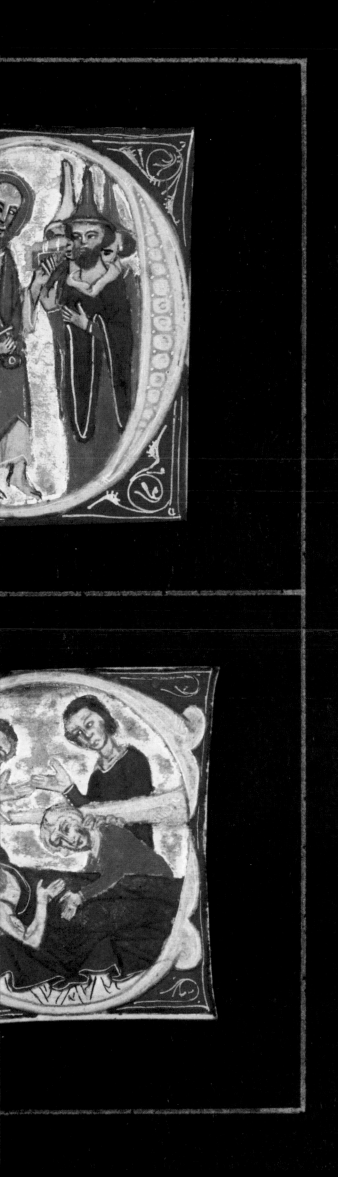

THE CONSTANTINOPLE EFFECT

In the scriptoria of Constantine's Constantinople were preserved many of the traditional features of manuscripts from late antiquity and early Christianity. Mixed with this classical influence was a strong oriental influence, which is not surprising, given Constantinople's position on the edge of Asia Minor.

The oriental influence shows particularly in the finest codices produced in the Eastern Roman Empire in the fifth and sixth centuries. These were richly coloured and luxuriously decorated, their lettering done in gold and silver, and the vellum on which they were written often dyed different colours, a rich imperial purple for really important works, intended, perhaps, for the emperor himself, or crimson for books which were to have gold texts. Saffron was also used to dye vellum yellow.

During the reign of the Emperor Justinian, who was educated at Constantinople and whose reign in the sixth century is renowned as the most brilliant in the history of the Empire, the art of book decoration reached a zenith. The gold ink, a famous feature of Byzantine book decoration, was made from gold especially imported from India, and rich artists' colours, including glorious vermilion and ultramarine, came from India, Persia and Spain.

The style of art which developed in the Eastern Roman Empire, centred on Constantinople, is known as 'Byzantine' art. It had a strongly religious and theological character and, because its main purpose was the instruction of the faithful, it was impersonal in style, very traditional in approach and highly stylized, whether the art was for the walls of churches or the illustrations in books. Unlike the art of its near neighbour Greece in the days of its glory, Byzantine art was not about humanity. Thus, very few Byzantine artists have been identified by name or by any individuality of style because the Byzantine artist knew better than to express his own feelings or to introduce any innovations into his work.

Despite this discipline, or perhaps because of it, the influence of Byzantine art spread far beyond the Eastern Roman Empire, showing particularly strongly in Russian religious art, especially icons, but also in Celtic illuminated manuscripts

Opposite: A series of 24 historiated initials and roundels from a Bible probably illuminated at Bologna. Italy, mid-13th century.

and, perhaps most significantly, in the renaissance of learning inspired by Charlemagne in western Europe in the eighth and ninth centuries.

CAROLINGIAN BOOK PRODUCTION

Charlemagne's imperial coronation in 800 is seen by many historians as the real beginning of the Middle Ages, as a great milestone on the road out of the darkness which had descended on the intellectual life of western Europe after the eclipse of the Roman way of life. Not that it was the way of life of classical Rome that Charlemagne was intent on reviving; rather, he wanted the intellectual life of his empire to be a recreation of the ferment of learning and thought which had characterized the first centuries of the Christian church.

Thus, much of the work that occupied the court schools and monastic scriptoria of the Carolingian period was concerned with reproducing and copying as accurately as possible authentic early Christian manuscripts written in Latin and Greek. Charlemagne brought scholars and artists from all over Europe to work in his schools and scriptoria; important though they were in their own right, however, Aachen, Tours, Metz, Rheims, the monastery of St Gall and the other great Carolingian schools, all drew inspiration from the court of Charlemagne and his successors.

There were other sources of inspiration for the many superb codices produced in the Carolingian period, of course, notably the scholars and artists from outside the Frankish kingdom that Charlemagne and his successors employed. Artists working in the Hellenistic Byzantine style and the style of Christian Rome are known to have worked in the Carolingian court schools, as did scholars and artists from Ireland, Northumberland and Spain.

Like the Franks themselves, the Irish, English and Spanish were descended, at least in part, from people whose work had been influenced by the art of the barbarian hordes who had invaded the western provinces of the crumbling Roman Empire. Decorated initials, for example, found their way into

Rightt: Books of hours were private devotional books, greatly prized by the nobility and the rich of Europe. By the 15th century, some time before this Book of Hours of the Virgin was made, less gorgeously illuminated, and therefore less expensive, versions could be bought in shops. Florence, Italy, c.1500.

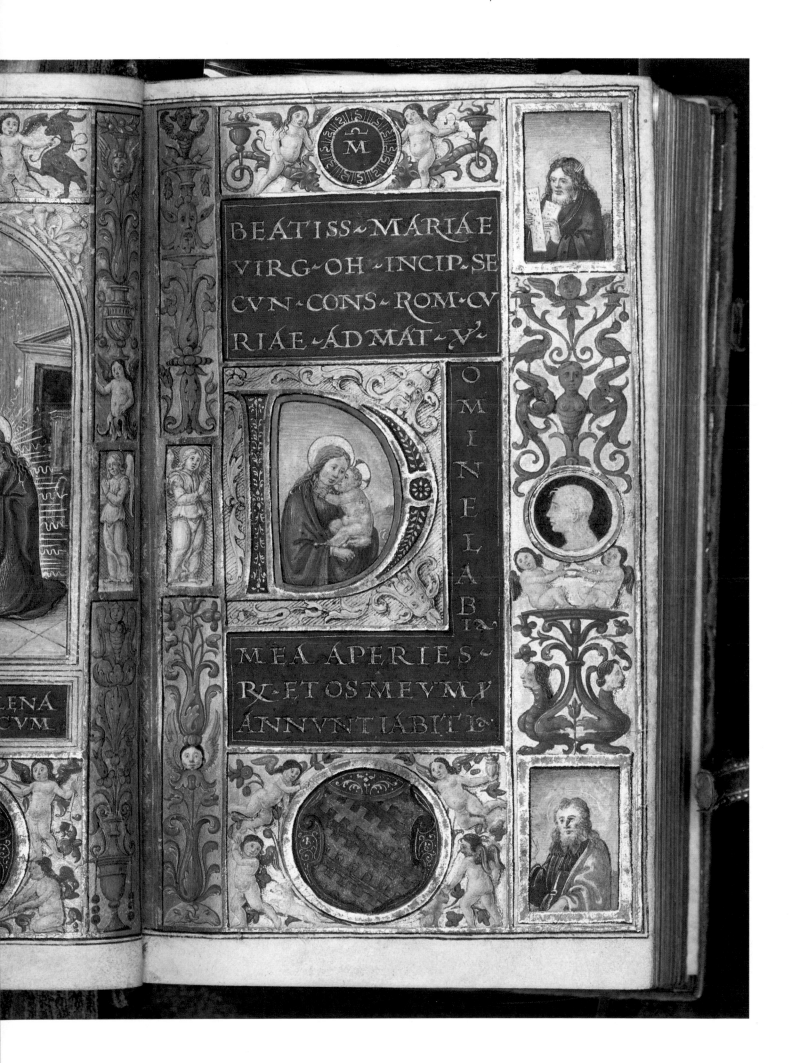

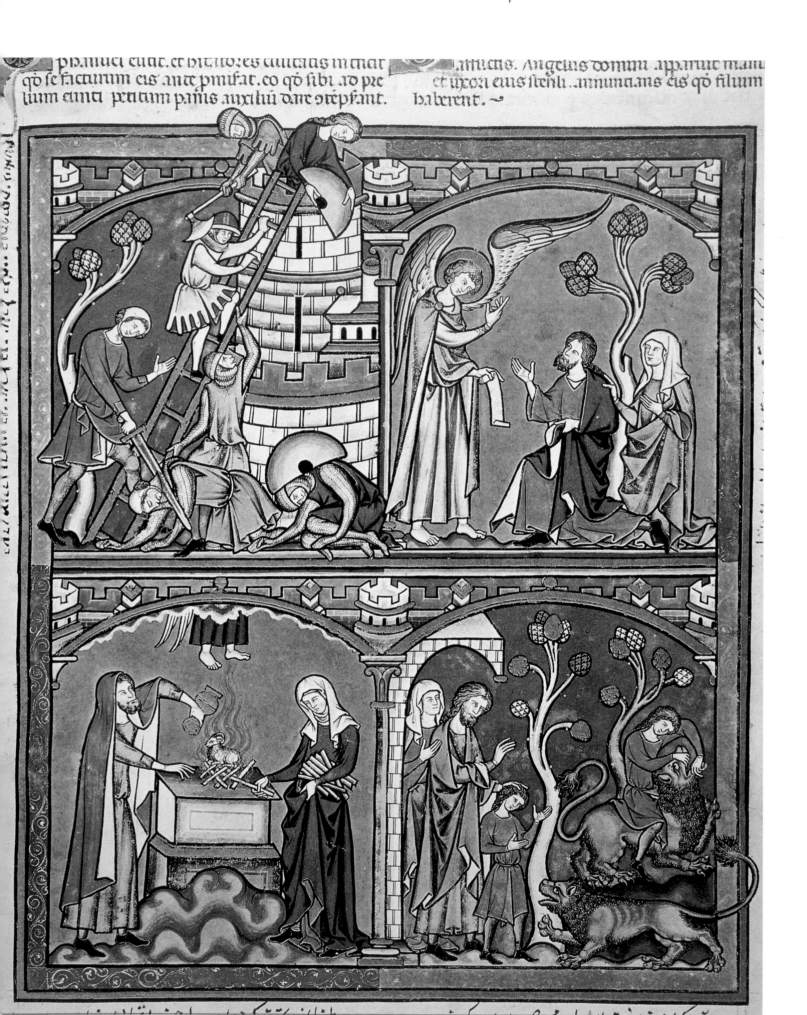

licet. N. mic
quibuf affai
cuncte ple
flaminiuz
N. moderati
folum cogno
nitatem &
cor yfdem
grauuuf com
& in aluud
fum eft de fe
Hoc. N. one
iam urgenti
& te me ipi

...ite siquid ego adiuto· curamue
leuasso: Que nuc te coqt &
uersat sub pectore fixa· & q
de primeris equide erit pmi
ysdem te affari uersibus attice
ur flaminiu ille uir aut magna
s fidei qquaz certe scio no ut
solicitari te noctescp diescp noui
n animi tui & eqtatem tecp no
n athenis deportasse: Sed huma
rudentiam intelligo: Et tn suspi
bus te quibus me ipum interdiuz
ueri quaz cosolatio & maior est
us differenda: Nuc aut mihi ui
ectute aliquid adte coscribere:
quod mihi tecum comune e: aut
aut certe aduentatis est senectus
leuari uolo: & site quide id mo

European illuminated manuscripts via Irish monks, whose art was strongly influenced by Celtic art. In fact, it was the fusion of the classical and the barbaric forms, particularly the Insular style, that enabled Carolingian book art to develop what became the characteristic forms of medieval illumination.

Many of the people who came into the Carolingian court schools and scriptoria are thought to have brought original manuscripts with them, introducing their contents and the style of their decoration into the work of the Carolingian schools. The *Evangelistary of Godescalc* was commissioned by Charlemagne and his wife Hildegard and made at the palace school at Aachen c. 781, and is therefore a very early example

Above: An historiated initial from a choir book, depicting an important New Testament scene, the Presentation of Christ in the Temple. Pisa, Italy, *c.*1340.

Opposite: A decided Byzantine influence shows in this page from the Syriac Gospels, produced at the monastery of Zagba in the 6th century and taken to Florence, where it is now one of the treasure of the Biblioteca Laurenziana, in 1497. Mesopotamia, *c.*586.

Overleaf: Portraits of St Mark and St Luke, from the Gospels Book (or Evangelistary) of Godescalc who produced this superb book for Charlemagne and his wife Hildegard. Godescalc used gold and silver paint on purple vellum, the gold being used to signify the splendour of heaven and eternal life.

Above: A fourteenth-century depiction of the Adoration of the Magi.

Opposite: A large historiated M, depicting the death of St Dominic, from a late medieval manuscript made in Bologna. Italy, c.1265.

Overleaf: The Fountain of Life, as depicted in the superb Gospels of Saint Médard of Soissons. Palace School, Aachen, early 9th century.

of a Carolingian illuminated manuscript. It has illustrations which reflect the art of paintings in Rome churches done earlier in the century, but also shows the influence of Insular art in the interlacing decoration at the top and bottom of pages. In contrast, the art which influenced the very beautiful *Coronation Gospels of the Holy Roman Empire*, made at the palace school in Aachen before 800, is clearly in the Hellenistic tradition of Byzantine artists.

Among the most important of the scholars who worked for Charlemagne was Alcuin of York, a great English scholar and master of the cloister school at York, who was invited to

join Charlemagne's court at Aix-la-Chapelle as tutor to the royal family. Eventually, Alcuin became abbot of the great abbey at Tours, the school he founded there becoming one of the most important in Europe. Alcuin's own writings, which included poetry, theological and ethical treatises, lives of the saints, and books on grammar, rhetoric and dialectic provided much of the material for the scribes and artists at Tours to work on.

Alcuin's main concern about the codices produced under his rule was that their texts should be as authentic and as accurate as possible. Indeed, one of the earliest instructions he received from Charlemagne was to prepare a correct version of the Bible, a task which occupied scholars, including advisers from Syria and Greece, many years.

Alcuin himself prepared a revised version of the Vulgate Bible, which had been the first Latin version of the Bible texts, authorized by the Council of Trent and made by St Jerome in the fourth century. A very fine example of Alcuin's version of the Vulgate Bible, believed to have been made at Tours as a coronation gift for Charlemagne, is in the British Library.

Decoration did not become an important part of books produced at Tours until a generation after Alcuin's death: then, the great one-volume Bibles produced at Tours, such as the *Moutier-Granval Bible* produced in 834-43 and now in the British Library, became items of wonder and awe, setting a standard for what Bibles should be for the whole of the early Middle Ages.

With so many schools, scriptoria and other centres of learning producing illuminated manuscripts during the Carolingian period, it is natural that many different styles and traditions of decoration and of interpreting the Bible stories should have developed. Overall, however, it can be said of the best Carolingian manuscripts, wherever they were made, that they have a splendid energy and a wonderfully outward-looking confidence.

OTTONIAN ART

Charlemagne's great empire turned out to be a frail thing. His successors were unable to keep control of the great lords of the empire, so that civil war became a destructive force where learning and education had been a binding one. Then, in the second half of the ninth century, Norse invaders began taking an interest in the Carolingian empire, which had neither an army on land nor a fleet at sea to counter them. Emperor

Charles III made a treaty with the Norsemen so disliked by his subjects that he was deposed in 887, and Charlemagne's empire split into pieces.

While many of the Carolingian monastery scriptoria and palace schools disappeared in the turmoil of the age, the scriptorium at Tours producing no work after a Norse invasion in 853, the influence of their work continued to be felt throughout Europe. While the civil fabric of Charlemagne's empire disintegrated, the Christian church proved much stronger, keeping its head down, as it were, and continuing to operate quietly in abbeys and monasteries where the traditions of the earlier age were still followed.

This was particularly so in the parts of Charlemagne's old empire beyond the Kingdom of the Franks in Germany. Thus when, after more than half a century of confusion and turmoil, the strong figure of the Saxon Henry the Fowler, who became the Emperor Henry I, emerged to fight back invaders from east and west, he found many centres where he could establish a revival of learning, a matter as important to the future of his empire as it had been to Charlemagne's. Now and during the reigns of the Emperors who followed, abbeys at Reichenau, Regensburg, Trier, Augsburg, Speyer, Bamberg, Basle and Echternach took on the mantle of book production last worn by the Carolingians.

This German artistic revival in the Holy Roman Empire takes its name, 'Ottonian', from the fact that three of Henry I's immediate successors were called Otto. Otto I was crowned king of the Germans at Aachen in 936, lifted the siege of Augsburg in 955, and was crowned Emperor at Rome in 962.

While there was as much variety in the artistic decoration of books under the Ottonian emperors as there was in the

Right: The Holy Roman Emperor Frederick II was both a great patron of the book and a writer of them, particularly poetry, too. This portrait dates from the 16th century.

Overleaf: The Roman Emperor Nero, is shown in a walled orchard from Pliny the Elder's version of *Historia Naturalis*. Italy.

De A. Theuet, Liure IIII. 247
FRIDERIC EMPEREVR II. DV NOM.
Chapitre 17.

quidem arbitr

A tura a
ra mario
prouenie
Restat e
manis in
uerus q̃
prius mi
quare tu
ra pro i
sessas a fo
te cum l
ca caduc
ca pendei
cum alit
delitiaru
nisse cla

N celle annee mesme q̃ ces
choses aduindzēt mourut le
roy loys Enterre fut en lab
baye saint remy de rains.
Tous les iours de sa bie bsa en angoisse
q en tribulacion. Deux filz eut de la royne
engeberge la seur othon qui depuis fut em
pereur Lothaire q charles. Et icelui char
les mena sa bie en priuees besongnes. Lo
thaire laisne couronnerē les barōs a raid
deuāt les ydes de nouembre En celle
annee mourut gilbert le duc de bourgon

time of the Carolingians, there were aspects of this German revival that are distinctively Ottonian. On the whole, book art under the Ottos and Henry II and Henry III, had a certain overall solemnity and seriousness, demonstrating a hieratic view of society, particularly in those manuscripts in which the emperors themselves were depicted – and there were quite a few of these, since the Ottonians were great patrons of book production.

It can also be said of the finest Ottonian illuminated manuscripts that while their initials, frames and other ornaments were particularly beautiful and their colours wonderfully rich, their human figures were, on the whole, not very good: too many artists seemed unable to cope with the subtleties of drawing hands and feet, or of drawing believable faces.

Strong influences on Ottonian book art came from Italy, where Otto I was the ruling political force, from Rome itself, still a main pilgrimage site in the early Middle Ages as well as a storehouse of early Christian relics and art, and from the Byzantine eastern empire.

A greatly increased knowledge of recent Byzantine art was brought to Otto II's court school at Cologne through Otto's marriage to the Princess Theophano, daughter of the Byzantine emperor, Romanes II, in 963. The princess brought to Germany Greek fashions and Greek artists, awakening in local artists an enthusiasm for adding details in the Byzantine style to the decorations on their manuscripts. The Byzantine tradition also showed in Ottonian illuminated manuscripts in the increased use of gold in backgrounds and in a subtle move away from naturalism in the depiction of human figures to a more two-dimensional, monumental treatment.

Nor had the influence of the Carolingian schools been lost. Under the Emperor Henry III, notable for sacking three popes in one year during his determined reformation of the papacy, the work of the abbey of Echternach came to the fore. Henry visited Echternach with his mother, the Empress Gisela, early in his reign and was greatly impressed by the lavishly decorated books produced in its scriptorium, which held manuscripts from several Carolingian schools, including Tours.

Henry commissioned a great number of books from Echternach, including the splendid *Codex Aureus* of Speyer, made at Echternach in 1045-46. There is even a commemoration of Henry's visit in a *Book of Pericopes* made at Echternach in about 1039, which includes a charming miniature of the Empress Gisela visiting Echternach, supported by the abbot and a crowd of courtiers.

The importance of royal and other patronage on book production is emphasized by the fact that after Henry III died in 1056, the scriptorium at Echternach soon began producing much smaller and less lavish books, the artistic quality of which also showed a marked decline.

THE ROMANESQUE STYLE

By the time of Henry III's death, the influence of the Byzantine tradition had waned and illuminated manuscript production at this latter end of the early medieval period in Europe took on much the same strongly stylized aspect, with little naturalism or humanism about it, characteristic of architecture at the time.

It is a style that has come to be called 'Romanesque', meaning in general a style based on a reapplication to art and architecture of the principles and designs of Roman architecture, but applied in particular to European architecture and the minor arts in the eleventh and twelfth centuries. Looking specifically at illuminated manuscripts of the period, the Romanesque style did not appear suddenly from nowhere. Rather, it developed naturally from the work of French, English and German book scribes and illuminators in the tenth century, a period of great monastic reform throughout Europe.

The emphasis on linear outline and an idealized rather than a natural depiction of the human form was characteristic of illuminated manuscripts in the late eleventh and early twelfth centuries. It grew partly out of the church's soul-searching over how far the human form, especially that of religious and Biblical figures, should be represented naturally in art. Would too realistic a depiction lead to the images themselves being venerated, rather than being seen as symbols? It was a debate that would have considerable influence of the work of manuscript illuminators in France, England, and the Netherlands, in particular, as the Romanesque period gave way to the Gothic and to the richest period of manuscript illumination in Europe.

Opposite: An obviously aristocratic figure, mounted on a plumed horse, at the head of an army is met outside a city by peasants and nobility alike. From the *Chroniques de France*. 1493.

CELTIC
IRELAND AND
ENGLAND

In the pre-medieval period in Europe, before the development of the Carolingian style, a unique style of manuscript illumination developed in Celtic Ireland and England, quite different from anything else in Europe. Based originally on the barbaric art and culture of Celtic Ireland, it grew into a beautiful and sophisticated art that was to have as important an influence on the art of manuscript illumination in Europe as the Byzantine style. It is known as the 'Insular' style.

Above: Portrait of St Patrick, the most important Christian missionary to Ireland, from the popular 18th-century work, Butler's Lives of the Saints.

Opposite: Canon Table – tables of concordance for the Gospels – from the Book of Kells. The tables from the 4th century and had been appearing for some two centuries before the Book of Kells artist set out his tables.

CHRISTIANITY IN IRELAND

The Christianization of Ireland is believed to have begun as early as the fourth century, though the first Christian missionary known by name was Palladius, who was sent to Ireland by the Pope in 430. St Patrick's mission in Ireland began about 455.

These early bringers of the Christian message found a well-established Celtic society in Ireland, divided into about 100 small kingdoms. The Celts, a barbaric people who had infiltrated Ireland from central Europe by way of western Europe and were well established by 500BC, had a strong oral culture and a rich artistic tradition, showing itself in their woven fabrics, stone carving and metalwork. These were notable for being done in a style based on geometrically woven patterns, in which naturalistic representations of plants, animals and human figures did not feature.

LATINE CANTICA CANTICORVM

VOX ECCLESIE DESIDE RANTIS ADUENTU XPI.

Above: An illuminated letter from the Old Testment's *Song of Solomon*, from the Winchester Bible. England, *c*.1150-1180.

Opposite: The Celtic Insular style of illumination at its most daring and subtle: Eight Circle Cross from the *Book of Kells*. Insular, after 800.

Overleaf: Extracts from the *Lindisfarne Gospels*, made at the monastery of Lindisfarne in Northumbria. England, *c*. 698.

Within a century of St Patrick's mission, monasticism was so well established in Ireland that historians are able to talk about the start of a 'golden age'. In Ireland's monasteries there were scribes copying manuscripts and codices brought to Ireland by the early missionaries to help them in their work. Gradually, styles based on local tradition found their way in the scribes', copiers' and decorators' work. Thus, when St Columba, whose name in Irish is 'Colmcille', meaning 'dove', took the Christian mission to the British Isles in the middle of the sixth century, founding monasteries on Iona and in the Hebrides, he would have been able to take with him gospels and other texts done in what was already an uniquely beautiful style.

St Columba had been educated at a monastery at Durrow (the remains of which may be seen today near Tullamore in County Offaly). It was at Durrow that one of Ireland's earliest known illuminated manuscripts, the seventh-century *Book of Durrow*, a superbly decorated copy of the four gospels, was made.

This beautiful book demonstrates to perfection the fact that by this period, Celtic illuminated manuscripts had a quality and style of decoration like no other in Europe. Not only did the manuscripts made in Ireland at this time make use of traditional patterns long employed in Celtic weaving and

61

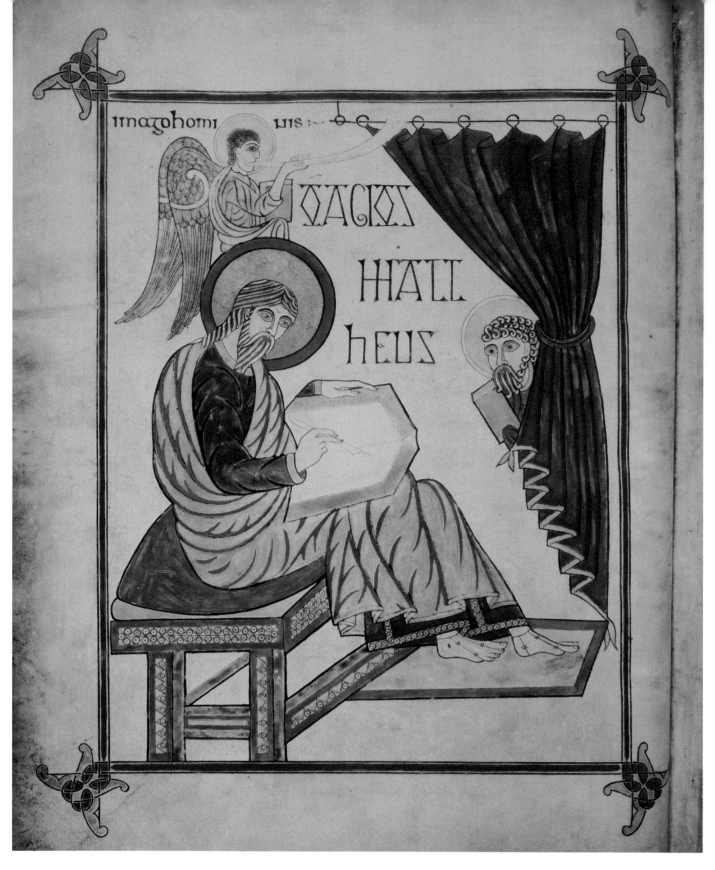

imagohomi uis :~

SACKS
HATT
heus

Above: St Matthew, as depicted in the Lindisfarne Gospels. England, c .698.

Opposite: A page from one of the oldest Celtic Insular Gospel Books, the Book of Durrow. Gospels books were one of the most important liturgical books at this time, because they were essential aids for missionaries. Ireland, c.680.

embroidery, metalwork and stone carving, but they also drew on the pre-Christian Celts' wonderfully rich heritage of folk-lore, in which so many stories and legends of the great Celtic warriors and kings were enlivened with accounts of mythic monsters, dragons, serpents, dogs and strange birds.

Legend has it that St Columba himself had a hand in the making of early medieval Ireland's most richly decorated man-uscript, the *Book of Kells*. It is easy to weave legends round this breathtaking book, however, since we do not know for certain where it was made. St Columba comes into the story because

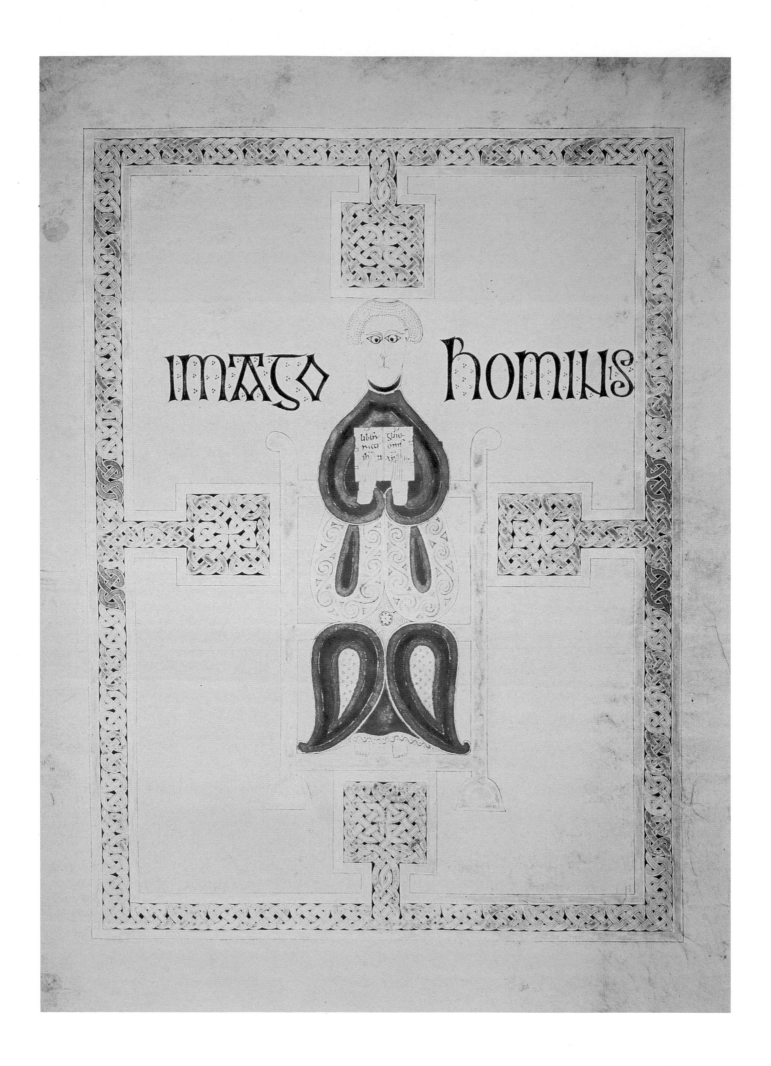

it is thought that the *Book of Kells* may have been made in his own monastery on Iona, and taken for safety to Kells early in the ninth century, when Viking raids on the west coast of Scotland and its islands were a constant threat.

The *Book of Kells* is another gospels book, its Latin text written in a rounded Celtic script embellished with intricately interlaced and richly coloured spirals. Animals, birds and human figures decorate the ends of many of the lines of text and are used symbolically in the decorations and initials. Symbolic illustrations of the four evangelists – Matthew, Mark, Luke and John – appear throughout the book.

The decorated initials in the *Book of Kells* are extraordinarily complex in their design, a reminder that the decorated initials which are such a feature of later European illuminated manuscripts, actually have their origins in the barbaric Celtic art of Ireland, and not the art of classical antiquity. While some of the frames and borders in these Celtic books hint at Byzantine

Above: A kneeling knight prays to a snail: a typically quirky border detail, or 'drollery', from the Gorleston Psalter, which is lively with genre motifs and scenes from daily life. England, early 14th century.

Opposite: The monogram of St Matthew, 'Imago hominus', from a Gospels book made at Echternach.

models – and it is possible that the early missionaries brought Byzantine manuscripts to Ireland – it should be noticed that neither the *Book of Durrow* nor the *Book of Kells* make use of gold, an important feature in Byzantine manuscripts, which was not available in Ireland at this time.

By the time the *Book of Kells* was made, Irish missionaries were taking the Christian message, and their books, into Europe. Wherever they stopped and worked, often establish-

ing monasteries — St Gall near Lake Constance, which became particularly famous for its illuminated manuscripts in Carolingian times, began as a cell established by a disciple of St Columba in 614 — they had a strong influence on the work of the scriptoria they worked in. The Irish style can be traced in monasteries along the Rhine, in Burgundy, in Switzerland and down into northern Italy.

ILLUMINATED MANUSCRIPTS IN EIGHTH-CENTURY ENGLAND

By the eighth century, English book art, which had developed rapidly after the time of St Columba, had become, to quote one historian, 'second to no other country in the Christian world'. By this time, Northumberland and the north of England were particularly rich in monasteries with several active scriptoria and important libraries. Jarrow, Durham, Lindisfarne and York were all great centres of learning and scholarship and of book production, and they are thought to have had links with monasteries in the south, such as Oxford, St Albans, Westminster and Glastonbury.

One of the most precious books to have survived from this first period of manuscript illumination in England is the *Lindisfarne Gospels*, which was probably made a century before the *Book of Kells*. The *Lindisfarne Gospels* was the work of Abbot Eadfrith, who was bishop of Lindisfarne in Northumbria early in the eighth century. Eadfrith's manuscript was made in a particularly magnificent style, using gold in both its lettering and its decoration, because it was produced in honour of St Cuthbert, Lindisfarne's most famous and holiest bishop, who had died in 687.

The Viking invasions which had caused such turmoil in Scotland and Ireland in the ninth century also greatly affected monastic life in England, particularly for those places established too near the coasts or on navigable rivers. Jarrow, for instance, founded in 681 and the monastery where the scholar and historian St Bede spent his whole life, was repeatedly sacked and repeatedly refounded, finally becoming a cell of

Left: Fragment from a gospel lectionary, a selection of passages from the Gospels to be read during Mass, perhaps made at Canterbury. England, *c*.1000.

Durham Cathedral. Lindisfarne, on its island off the Northumbrian coast, was so vulnerable that its precious books, including the *Lindisfarne Gospels*, were taken to Durham for safe-keeping (along with the remains of St Cuthbert).

While the turmoil of the times reduced the activities of scriptoria and libraries, it did not stop them, so that the ninth century became a period of consolidation for English illuminators as well as a time of increased interaction with the monastic establishments of the Carolingian empire. This brought to the notice of English illuminators not only the work being done in Charlemagne's empire, but also many examples of Byzantine and Roman manuscripts. These were not so much copied by English scribes and illuminators as observed for forms and styles which could be adapted for what became an uniquely English style. Anglo-Saxon art, based on the fine drawing of graceful figures and lively decorations, delicately tinted, was used in the Carolingian style – that is, on pages were filled with figures and decoration.

Opposite: An elaborate border and opening capitals feature on the frontispiece of the Gospel of St Matthew, from the MacDurnan Gospels, made at the monastery of Armagh. Ireland, 9th century.

Below: The genealogy of Christ, as set out in the Book of Kells. In later manuscripts, the genealogy was often set out pictorially, in the form of the Tree of Jesse. Insular, after 800.

THE SECOND GREAT PERIOD OF ENGLISH ILLUMINATION

The tenth century saw the beginning of a great age of monastic reform in England which was to last until the beginning of the thirteenth century, relatively unhindered by the Norman Conquest: indeed, in the 35-year reign of William the Conqueror's son, the able and scholarly Henry I, some 150 religious houses were founded in England.

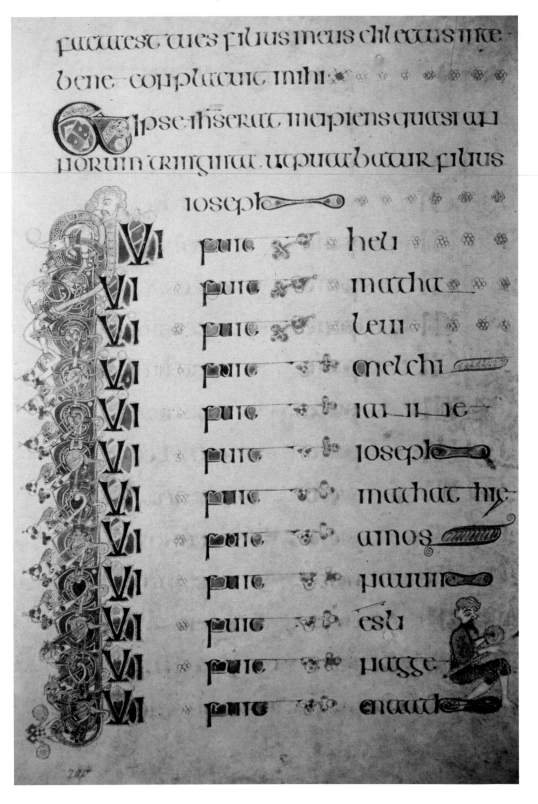

The dominant style in English illuminated manuscripts in the tenth century came from Winchester, capital of the Saxon kingdom of Wessex. Here, a New Minster had been founded by King Alfred's son, Edward, with its first charter being granted in 901. By mid-century, Winchester had come under the patronage of one of the great leaders of the monastic reform movement in England, St Ethelwold. As Bishop of Winchester, Ethelwold turned Winchester into an important centre of learning where many superb illuminated manuscripts were created in a style which the art historian Nikolaus Pevsner has called 'the first national style in English art'.

The Winchester style soon appeared in the work of other monastic scriptoria in southern England. This was partly because by this time both monks and lay scribes had begun travelling from one centre to another, offering their experience and abilities in a freelance capacity and partly because Ethelwold himself founded or refounded a number of monasteries, where his great interest in books and learning had a strong influence.

Several distinct elements can be found in the Winchester style. Frames and borders are enclosed in gold edgings, which project into ornamental bosses at the corners, and the frame decorations within the gold are heavy with acanthus-leaf foliage and climbing figures. Illustrations in Winchester manuscripts may be miniatures painted in opaque colours or outline pen drawings. Particularly distinctive in later Winchester school figures is the style of drapery, in which the folds are painted so that they look as if they are wet and clinging to the body – a style known as 'damp fold' drapery.

Such elements can be seen in Winchester school manuscripts from early on. The *Benedictional of St Ethelwold*, made between 971 and 984, is a richly decorated example of late Anglo-Saxon art at its best and makes lavish use of gold paint, including in the text. A Latin poem at the beginning tells us that Ethelwold commanded the making of the book that 'he might be able to sanctify the people of the Saviour by means of it and pour forth holy prayer

to God for the flock committed to him, and that he may lose no lambkin of the fold'.

The masterpiece of the Winchester school, the *Winchester Bible*, was worked on by six major artists, as well as other decorators and illuminators, between 1150 and 1180, though it was never completed. One of the artists is known as the Master of the Leaping Figures because of the masterly way he depicted figures in movement; another, the Master of the Aprocrypha Drawings, contributed full-page uncoloured line drawings in a wonderfully lively style.

The twelfth century, during which the Romanesque style was dominant throughout Europe, was a time of outstanding illuminated manuscript production in England. By

Above right: An illuminated letter from the Winchester Bible, which was the work of a team of artists including the renowned Master of the Leaping Figures. England, c.1150-1180.

Opposite: Ecclesia from Psalm 101, including a finely depicted church, from the East Anglian Gorleston Psalter. England, early 14th century.

now, the Norman kings' need for textbooks, rather than beautiful picture books, had been assuaged and, where text and decorative initials had once dominated, the miniature now came back into its own.

Outstanding examples of full-page miniatures in the Romanesque style can be seen in the superb *St Albans Psalter*, produced in the scriptorium at St Albans, one of the most important in England in the Middle Ages, between 1119 and 1123. The leading illuminator at St Albans in the first half of the twelfth century was an Englishman, Matthew Paris, who headed the scriptorium there and who was also a scholar and historian. However, it is believed that the 40 full-page miniatures which open the *St Albans Psalter* were the work of an artist known as the Alexis Master because of the drawings he did for a *Life of St Alexis* and whose influence was felt throughout English manu script production for many years.

ENGLISH ILLUMINATION AFTER THE GOTHIC PERIOD

While much English illumination of the thirteenth and early fourteenth centuries, particularly after the relatively sudden mid-century appearance of the Gothic style, is not easy to distinguish from French or Netherlands art of the same period, it still retained many features that were quintessentially English. There was a lively, humorous quality about it, with grotesque animals, drolleries and humorous scenes from everyday life allowed to work their way into and beyond the decorative borders and *bas de page* decorations. English illuminators even carried their enthusiasm for filling the margins of their pages

Previous pages left: This elaborately bordered initial B from the Peterborough Psalter contains two pictures within its curves: Christ seated (top) and two women representing Mercy and Truth (bottom). England, c. 1260.

Previous pages right: Tree of Jesse, depicting the genealogy of Christ, from Isaiah in the Lambeth Bible, made at Caterbury. England, c.1140-50.

Opposite: A page from the *Historia Anglorum*, by Matthew Paris, who was in charge of the scriptorium at St Albans Abbey for many years. Matthew Paris has included himself in the picture, kneeling in homage to the Virgin and Holy Child. England, 13th century.

into the extensions of initials, so that they too reached out into the margins.

These qualities show in manuscripts, mostly psalters, produced in East Anglian scriptoria early in the fourteenth century, and in such books as the *Arundel Psalter*, made early in the fourteenth century and enlivened with many amusing drolleries and some very fine pen drawing.

The end of the fourteenth century saw a final flourish in the production of illuminated manuscripts in England. A royal marriage, involving a beautiful and charming European princess who became very popular in England, brought it about. Richard II's first wife was Anne of Bohemia, daughter of the Emperor Charles IV, who was also king of Bohemia. Charles established at Prague, his Bohemian capital, a new university and an important school of illumination, whose artists, many of them French and Italian, produced such great works as the well-known Vienna copy of the *Golden Bull of Charles IV* ordered by his son Wenzel in 1400 and the *Wenzel Bible*.

When his daughter Anne came to England to marry Richard, she brought a large retinue of fashionable and stylish Bohemians with her, as well as artists and many examples of their work. Just as the fashionable Bohemians had an effect on English dress style – they soon had Englishmen wearing extraordinary shoes with points so long they had to be tied up to the wearer's legs (with silver chains if the wearer was intent on being at the forefront of fashion) – so the artists from Bohemia had an effect on English illuminated manuscripts.

The most noticeable change was in the inclusion of foliage and flowers in the Bohemian style in English-produced manuscripts; these became luxuriant, softly curled and delicately coloured and appeared in initials and in border decorations. Another change attributable to Bohemian influence was the way in which English artists began shifting away from painting faces in a long, colourless style, in the French manner, to making them plump and ruddy – more like real people, in fact.

During the fifteenth century, the native style of manuscript illumination in England faltered before waves of continental influence, Flemish in particular. Then, of course, there was the matter of the introduction of printing, William Caxton setting up his first English printing press in Westminster in 1476. By the end of the century, book illumination in England was neither creative nor extensive; by the time Elizabeth Tudor came to the throne, it was history.

Ekaunt li aignel auen ouen le sume sel graunt
Ereremuet fu fet. E le solail fu fet neir ausi cum un
sac de peil. e tote la lune su fer cum sanc. e les esteile del
cel cheuent sur la tere. ausi cum le fier lest cheir sun faus truit
kaunt il est mu de graunt uent. E le cel sen departi cū un
linere enuolupe. ꝫ chekeune muntaine e les isles sunt
remues de lur liu. E les reise les princes. e les bailiffi. e les
riches e les fors. e les serfs. e les frauns semuiterent en
fosel. e en peres des muntaines. E dirent as muntaines.
e as peres. Cheez sur nus. e musceris nus de la fate al se
aunt sur le throne. e del curus del aignel. pur ço ke le
graunt iur de lur curus uent. E ki purra ester.

Le ouerture del sume sel aparteint al derecer des guis e a la
pel des paens. Il oueri le sume sel kaunt il pempli poeuere
ço ke il auen auaunt dist. Grauit te moc. par la tere en test liu. les
guis fut signetez. Teremor est fet. kaunt teste gent fut destruz p les
romeins. Li solail é fet neir. kaunt les guis. ki par conusaunce
de un sul deu. e p la garde de lai resplendoient entre gent cū le
solail. e pus fut haut de rote gēt pur lur felonies. La lune sig
netie le synagoge. ke est cū sanc del sanc ihu crist. par les este
les. les princes del prestre. e les notaries e les pharisens sunt enten
duz p le cel. le ueu testamēt. ki paser des guis treske a paeins.
P les muntanes. ceus ki manenient en la citez p les isles. cē ki mane
ient es chaumpestres. P les reis e les bailiffi. cē ki gouernerent le po
ple.

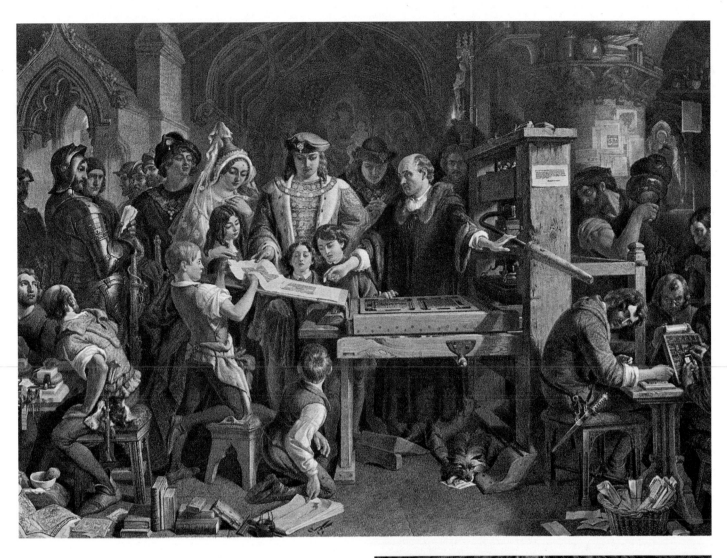

Above: A 19th-century rendition of the great moment in English history when Caxton showed the first specimen of his printing to King Edward IV at Westminster.

Right: This fine study of Queen Elizabeth I kneeling in prayer was the frontispiece to *Christian Prayers*, a book produced in England in 1569.

Opposite: 'Choirs of Angels' fill this page from the Anglo-Norman Trinity Apocalypse, a lavishly illustrated version of the Book of Revelation, with a text in French. England, 13th century.

A Golden Age
1150~1350

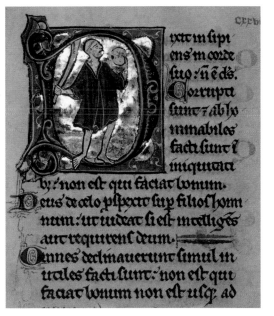

Europe in the twelfth, thirteenth and fourteenth centuries was a continent in transition. Subtle shifts in the balance of power between states were taking place, so that the German Empire, the strongest state in the twelfth century, was having to yield influence in Italy and to France. There was also a greater movement of people between one country and another. Where once the Church had been the only real international organization in Europe, Latin-speaking monks born in one country moving easily into monasteries of their order in other countries, now there were other groups of people on the move.

Foremost among these were the men – architects,

builders, stonemasons, wood carvers – who built the great cathedrals of Europe, many of them in an ornate style, first seen in France in the thirteenth century and characterized by pointed arches, elaborate tracery and flying buttresses which later came to be called Gothic. These people were a real freemasonry, taking their skills anywhere in Europe they could be used. Moving in their wake were many itinerant artists, ivory carvers, jewellers and other specialists in the minor arts – including, of course, secular practitioners of the art of manuscript illumination, many of them with pattern books in their baggage.

As in politics, so in the intellectual and artistic life of society, the secular world was eating into the dominance of the Church. It was not just that the Church hierarchy at the end of the Middle Ages was having to make concessions, deciding at the Fourth Lateran Council in 1215, for instance, that private devotion ought to be encouraged amongst the laity – a ruling which led to a great increase in the production of psalters and books of hours. The Church, despite the great

stationers' shops in university towns and cities where books could be bought by burghers and students — provided, it must be admitted, they were rich enough.

When Ethelwold became Bishop of Winchester in 963, one of his earliest actions had been to eject all the secular clergy from the cathedral and from the New Minster school, replacing them with monks. While many of these monks were brilliant illuminators, as we know from the superb manuscripts they and their successors at Winchester produced, their first duty, like that of monks anywhere in the Christian world, was always to God: everything in their lives, which was ruled by the need for humility, was dedicated to giving glory to God.

Whatever else they did in life, whether eating their simple and frugal meals, working in their monastery's fields, inscribing texts, or decorating them, monks had to fit everything into a day dominated by the necessity of observing the eight offices or hours into which it was divided, from Matins, as early as midnight or two in the morning, to Vespers at sunset, then Compline, which ended the day.

Now, a couple of centuries after Ethelwold, the outside world was finding its way into these enclosed communities, letting in the heady scent of life as it was lived by ordinary people. At the same time, secular artists and craftsmen were setting up their own guilds and fraternities which offered their members protection and regular work; it became common for guild apprentices to move away from their home towns to gain experience in guilds elsewhere.

monastic movements of the eleventh and twelfth centuries, was also having to let the outside world into its own domains.

At the same time, other centres of intellectual excellence, especially universities — Bologna, Paris and Oxford were all established in the early twelfth century — were challenging the positions of the Church and the ruling classes as the only sources of learning and thought. More and more people were learning to read and write, and were demanding books of all kinds, not just theological and liturgical texts. Their demands were increasingly met by secular book producers, setting up

Another force for change, which was to have a great effect on manuscript decoration, came with the birth of Francesco Bernardone in Italy c. 1181. As St Francis of Assisi, he is revered as the man who brought simple belief in faith and penitence into Christian belief. His bands of roving preachers, formed into the Friars Minor, took the message of poverty, humbleness and evangelical freedom through much of Europe, carrying with them illustrated Bible texts, including *Bibles moralisées*, those strip cartoons of the medieval world.

The significance of the familiar picture of St Francis feeding the birds lies in the fact that he was reminding Christians everywhere that religion was about more than praising God: nature had a place in it, too, for St Francis taught the importance of preserving God's world, in all its beauty and abundance. He thus helped widen the horizons of book artists, showing them that the works of nature — plants and flowers, animals and landscapes — could, and should, be used in their art. (There was good reason for

Above: The Holy Roman Emperor, Frederick I, surnamed Barbarossa, and his sons: a contemporary portrait from the German Weingarten Chronicles, 1179-91.

Opposite: Adam naming the beasts: from the Aberdeen Bestiary, a manuscript made in the North Midlands. England, 12th century.

Left: A typically vivid scene, packed with detail, showing an assault on a Saracen city, from a 14th-century version of Froissart's Chronicles.

Pope John Paul II's proclamation of St Francis of Assisi as patron saint of ecologists in 1979).

PAINTING THE HUMAN FIGURE

Illuminated manuscripts of the late medieval period in Europe – to about 1350 – showed more regional variations in style in the early years than by the mid-fourteenth century, by which period the great changes taking place in European life and thought had begun to change the illuminators' approach to their art.

Figurative art moved towards a more realistic portrayal of the human body. This gradual change was helped by the fact that by the end of the twelfth century the hierarchy of the Church had overcome its great worry that a too-human style for Biblical figures, whether as sculpture, carving, or drawing, might lead people to venerate the figures for themselves and not as symbols.

Now, the human figure as portrayed in illuminated manuscripts moved from the rather stocky and static approach of the Romanesque style to the taller and willowy figure characteristic of early Gothic art. If a picture included several figures, they would now be drawn to relate to each other, rather than being set stiffly apart.

The famous St Louis Psalter, made for Louis IX of France some time after 1250, contains 78 small, delicately tinted miniatures, showing the beginning of a new style in illuminated manuscripts. Gone is the 'damp-fold drapery', replaced by drapery

Opposite: Abraham and the Three Angels, framed in a richly ornamental border, including trailing vines: one of 78 delicately painted miniatures in the St Louis Psalter, made for King Louis IX, later St Louis, of France. France, *c*.1250-70.

Below: A page from a Psalter made for Blanche of Castile, Queen of France and mother of Louis IX. Like the later St Louis Psalter, this includes work in a style transitional from monastic to Gothic. France, *c*.1220.

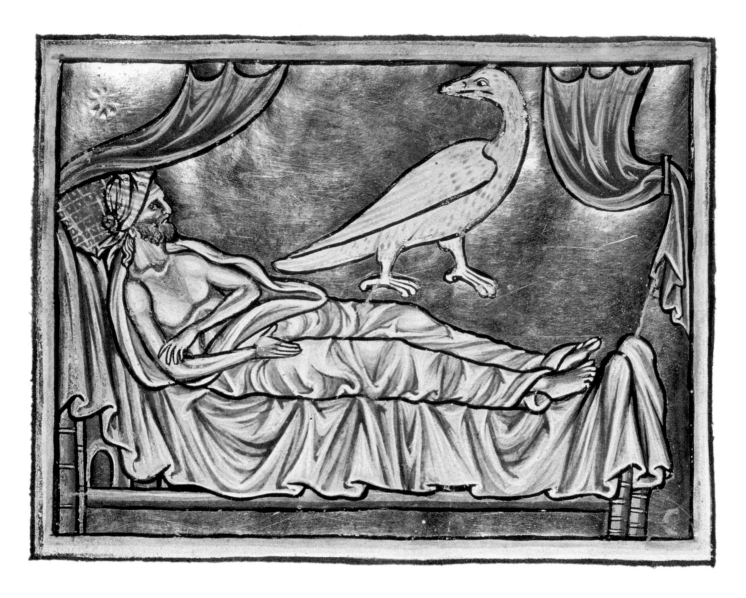

Above: Calandrius bird, from a Bestiary based on a 5th-century Physiologus and made at Durham. This bird was reputed to be able to foretell the fate of a sick man, hence its place above the man in bed. England, c.1200.

Opposite: Historiated initial B, depicting the birth of Christ, cut from an illuminated manuscript choirbook on vellum.

Overleaf left: Pentecost, one of 27 large miniatures in the Psalter of Ingeborg, made for Ingeborg, wife of Philip II of France. Tournai, France, early 13th century.

falling more naturally over figures which are graceful, slender and gentle, with a curving shape. By the end of the thirteenth century this curving of the figure had become a pronounced 'S' shape, seen at its most elegant in the well-known *Queen Mary Psalter*, made in England early in the fourteenth century.

The *Queen Mary Psalter* also highlights the way in which the depiction of faces and hair had also become much more natural and realistic. Wavy lines above the head have given way to hair and beards which look as if they have grown naturally on the heads and have been cut into individual styles, faces have been given individual features and there has been some attempt at drawing life-like expressions.

THE BEGINNINGS OF REALISM IN SETTINGS

Both the *St Louis Psalter* and the *Queen Mary Psalter* demonstrate that for the artists of this early Gothic period, contemporary architecture, sculpture and painted glass windows were important sources for backgrounds, settings and borders – and, indeed, for the S-bend posture of figures, which was common in the sculpture and ivory carving of the period.

By the beginning of the fourteenth century,

La pentecoste.

bunt. Ba. sicut sol in cospectu dei.

Mnipotens clementissime de9
qui sanctarum tuarum Mar-
the. margarete. barbare. apolonie et
katherine exaudisti prerogatiuamqꝫ
eis dedisti Da nobis per illarum inter-
cessiones in tribulationibus auxilium.
vt tibi regratiari valeamus. et tecum
in celis coronari . Qui viuis.

Septem psalmi penitentiales.

manuscript illuminators were becoming more like real artists rather than illustrators, giving their miniatures life-like settings, both indoors and out, and using perspective to give a three-dimensional effect to their work.

Particularly striking examples of an artist giving his work pictorial space can be seen in the work of Jean Pucelle, the main artist to the French court in the first half of the fourteenth century. He is thought to have been influenced by painting style in Italy and, certainly, his work brought a new life and dimension to French illuminated manuscripts.

Pucelle's *Bellville Breviary*, made in his workshop around 1325, has figures in architectural settings with three-dimensional space and also, in borders and margins, exquisitely drawn birds, animals, insects and flowers   fine observations of nature far from the grotesqueries or drolleries of earlier manuscripts.

The influence of the painted glass windows in Gothic cathedrals and churches on illuminated manuscripts can be seen at its most striking in *Bibles moralisées* made in Paris during Louis IX's reign and much copied thereafter. Manuscript designers transferred direct to their pages the rows of circular medallions, set one above the other in church windows, each medallion illustrating a different bible story or pointing the moral to be gained from it.

These Bibles and other manuscripts of the time were clearly influenced by the new way of thinking about and looking at the world which St Francis had started, and which was being stressed in the preachings of the Franciscan and Dominican friars. By now, monasteries no longer had exclusive rights to the production of art and literature, which meant that both art and literature were no longer confined very largely to religious texts. There were new subjects to inspire artists – history, poetry, romances, even students' text books – and to give the illuminated manuscript new subjects to turn into objects of beauty.

Previous page: Bees fly down to their hives in a miniature from the Aberdeen Bestiary. England, 12th century.

Left: An illuminated manuscript, perhaps made at Tours, combining alternating books of hours, in which scenes from *The Hours of the Virgin* alternate with scenes from the *Hours of the Cross* and the *Hours of the Holy Ghost*. France, c.1527.

Aries. leo. sagittarius. sunt
calida et sicca collerica
masculina. Orientalia.

Taurus. virgo. capricor
sunt frigida et sicca mel
lica feminina. Occident.

Gemini. aquarius.
libra. sunt calida et
humida masculina
sanguinea. occidentalia.

Cancer.
sunt frigida et
da flemmatica fe
na. Septentrionalia.

PATRONAGE AND THE MANUSCRIPT

None of the finest illuminated manuscripts was the work of an artist simply setting out to express himself in ink and paint. People of wealth and authority caused the manuscripts to be made, providing the funds that made not only the creation of the book possible, but also, in many cases, setting up and paying for the court schools, monastery scriptoria and ateliers in which they were made.

In many cases, the men and women commissioning these manuscripts interested themselves closely in the style and con-

Above: Emperor Frederick II (1194–1250) was a noted patron of the arts.

Opposite: Anatomical man, from a book of hours made for the Duc de Berry, with miniatures by Paul Limbourg. France, early 15th century.

tents of the work, perhaps specifying the saints to be listed in psalters and books of hours, or indicating how they wished to see themselves portrayed in the work, and even dictating the colours to be used, or the amount of gold with which the book should be embellished.

Whoever the patron, in the early Middle Ages most illuminated manuscripts were religious in content. Even so, there were many ways in which a secular patron could make his mark on the book. *Count Vivian's Bible*, produced at the Abbey of St Martin at Tours in the 840s, when Count Vivian was the abbey's lay abbot, was made for King Charles the Bald (hence its alternative name, *The First Bible of Charles the Bald*). It includes a splendidly lively miniature of the Count and his monks presenting the Bible to King Charles — one of the earliest pictures of an actual historical event known in medieval art in Western Europe.

Art historians see a double significance in *Count Vivian's*

Left: King David, from a book of hours from the Paris workshop of the Boucicant Master. France, *c.*1415.

Overleaf left: May: from one of the finest of Flemish illuminated manuscripts, the Tres Riches Heures du Duc de Berry, with illuminations by the Limbourg brothers. Flanders, *c.*1416.

Overleaf right: July, from the Limbourg Brothers' Tres Riches Heures du Duc de Berry. Flanders, *c.*1416.

Above: One of the great Renaissance patrons of the illuminated manuscript, Federigo da Montefeltro, Duke of Urbino, reads from a book in his library to his son Guidobaldo. From a painting by Pedro Berruguete, late 15th century.

Opposite: A fine Annunciation, from a book of hours made in northern France or in Flanders, c.1470.

Bible and the contemporary *Gospels of Lothair*, also made at Tours. The Emperor Lothair I, who was Charles the Bald's half-brother, and Charles are both depicted, seated crowned on their thrones, in finely idealised portraits in their respective books; it is as if some ninth-century public relations is going on here, with a particular political image of the Carolingian system being presented. The second significant point about these books lies in the fact that they represent an advance in the quality of the work being done at Tours at the time, as if it needed the spur of royal patronage to send it to greater heights of excellence.

The later Ottonian emperors were major patrons of the illuminated book, whose influence on book production extended to ordering master artists from one centre of their empire to another as they wished; an effect of this practice was to cause local styles of decoration to be influenced by artists from outside. The Ottonian rulers, like the Carolingians, were also good at ensuring that they themselves featured prominently in books produced under their patronage. Thus portraits of Otto II and Otto III, enthroned in majesty and receiving the homage of the fours parts of their empire, appear in several illuminated manuscripts, all of religious subjects, produced during their reigns.

At a time when women's cloisters in Germany and the Netherlands were very active centres of learning and book production, the female relatives of the three Ottonian emperors were outstanding among the book patrons of their day. Otto I's mother, Mathilda, was the patroness of several cloister-schools for women and also taught her own maids and servants to read. One of Otto's sisters, also called Mathilda, as Abbess of Quedlinburg commissioned a history of the two Saxons kings, her father Henry and her brother Otto. Otto I's wife, Adelheid of Burgundy, was in her youth an enthusiastic patron of the Abbey of Cluny and throughout her long life commissioned many illuminated books of poetry and theology, as well as paying for the liturgical books used in the various religious houses she founded.

Adelheid's patronage of poetry as well as of theological and liturgical books is an indication of how, as the Middle Ages progressed, patrons were widening their areas of interest. By the thirteenth century, patrons' interests, while still essentially founded in producing books with a religious or theological content, were beginning to be spread much wider.

The Holy Roman Emperor Frederick II – known as *Stupor*

Mundi, the Wonder of the World — was outstanding among thirteenth-century patrons. Not only did he encourage the work of artists, but he also wrote many books himself, notably poetry in Italian, one of several languages he spoke fluently. His great interest in natural science no doubt lay behind a book which is now one of the treasures of the Vatican Library, *De arte venandi cum avibus*. Frederick wrote the text for this book, and ordered the decoration, which included paintings of birds and hunting scenes.

In the thirteenth and fourteenth centuries, major centres of illuminated manuscript patronage were to be found round the English and French courts, where the sovereigns, their relatives and nobles connected to the court were all patrons. We have seen earlier how in the late fourteenth century, English style was influenced, though the marriage of Richard II to Anne of Bohemia, by the style practised at the court in Prague of the Holy Roman Emperors.

Patronage in Bohemia centred on the royal court, but also had other sources. The first Archbishop of Prague is known to have employed many scribes, but an even greater patron was secular. This was Gerhard Groot, founder in 1383 of the House of the Brothers of the Common Life, who made a very profitable business from transcribing books: one of their number is recorded as having been paid 500 gold gulden for a Bible. The Brothers took to wearing goose feather quills in their hats, which earned them the nickname of 'Brothers of the Pen'.

At the French court, Isabella of Bavaria, wife of Charles VI, was a great patron of the book, commissioning among many other books a stunningly beautiful version of the poems of the renowned poet, Christine de Pisan. And even more

Left: A Book of Hours of the Virgin, made for Catherine of Valois, who became Queen of England when she married Henry V. (France/England), early 15th century.

Overleaf left: Jacquemart de Hesdin, a celebrated illuminated manuscript artist, portrayed his patron, Jean, Duc de Berry, with St Andrew and St John, in the frontispiece to this Tres Belles Heures, commissioned by the duke. Flanders, early 15th century.

Overleaf right: Louis XII entering the city of Qenes, under a canopy and followed by four cardinals: miniature attributed to Jean Bourdichon in the Book of Hours of Anne of Brittany.

Above: Italian artists Taddeo Crivelli and Franco Rossi included this splendid banquet scene for the month of January in the Bible of Borso d'Este, Duke of Ferrara, one of the glories of Italian illuminated manuscript making. Italy, late 15th century.

Opposite: The Nativity, by Italian manuscript artist Da Crema, fills this historiated initial P, from a large-scale manuscript made in Lombardy. Italy, *c*.1490.

spectacular was the book commissioning activities of Jean, Duc de Berri, which are described in the next chapter.

A later French queen, Anne of Brittany, wife first of Charles VIII and then of Louis XII, was another noted patron of the book, one of the most celebrated of her commissions being the *Hours of Anne of Brittany*, now in the National Library of France in Paris. This superb example of French Renaissance illumination was made early in the sixteenth century, a paper in the royal archives recording that in 1508 Anne made an order for payment to the illuminator Jean Bourdichon of '1,050 *livres tournois*' for having 'richly and sumptuously historiated and illuminated a great Book of Hours for our use and service to which he has employed much time'.

By the fifteenth century, many of the outstanding patrons of the age were to be found in Italy, especially among the courts of the northern princes and in the court-like households of the great Italian bankers and merchants, such as the Medici of Florence.

The commissioning of religious books, even in the humanist age of the Renaissance, was still important. The great two-volume Bible commissioned by Borso d'Este, Duke of Ferrara, and illustrated in sumptuous style by Crivelli and

other artists, remains one of the outstanding achievements of Italian Renaissance illumination. For Borso d'Este, the commissioning of this great Bible probably had as much to do with personal prestige as with religious conviction, however, and it is true that for many Italian patrons, secular subjects were of as much interest as religious ones.

The two were mixed with splendid results in the funeral eulogy commissioned when the great Gian Galeazzo Visconti, Duke of Milan, died. This superbly illustrated manuscript included an illustrated family tree and a miniature of the duke being welcomed to heaven by the Virgin Mary and the Infant Christ.

For Federigo da Montefeltro, Duke of Urbino, his library and its books were the centre of his world. Among the 500 people at his court in Urbino, there were five men employed solely to read aloud at meals from books in his library and another four employed in transcribing manuscripts; elsewhere in Italy, he employed some 30 or 40 scribes copying manuscripts for him.

As Vespesiano wrote of him, 'He alone had a mind to do what no one had done for a thousand years or more; that is, to create the finest library since ancient times. He spared neither cost nor labour, and when he knew of a fine book, whether in Italy or not, he would send for it.' Federigo was indeed a paragon among patrons.

Opposite: A fifteenth-century depiction from the artist Bartholomaeus Anglicus (Nevers or Bourges) of astronomers contemplating the universe.

Below: The Medici Pope, Leo X, portrayed by Raphael with Giulio de' Medici and Cardinal Luigi de Rossi. This portrait was painted after 1513, when Giovanni de' Medici was chosen to succeed Julius II as Pope.

THE RENAISSANCE AND AFTER

Illuminated manuscripts provided the medieval world with some of its finest art, and continued to do so as the medieval world gave way to the modern, mirroring in their changes of subject, content and style the very great changes taking place in Europe in the fourteenth and fifteenth centuries. Where, in the early Middle Ages, the subject of most book illustration was religious, now, as the Renaissance in Italy was ushering in the modern world, illuminators were being given new texts to illustrate: history

Above: Title page from a late 16th century edition of the Vulgate Bible, printed in Latin. c. 1590.

Opposite: Fra Angelico, one of the greatest painters of Renaissance Florence, painted this historiated initial S, depicting the Presentation in the Temple, for a Missal. Italy, early 15th century.

by Froissart, poetry by Chaucer, Dante, Petrarch and Christine de Pisan, retellings of the ancient stories of King Arthur, the deeds of past heroes such as Alexander the Great and Charlemagne and his Paladins, and new writings on the sciences, including astronomy and, particularly in Italy, medicine and health.

Art was continuing to take the great strides away from its narrow medieval confines along a new path indicated by the Italian artists Cimabue, Martini and Giotto early in the fourteenth century. The social devastation caused by the Black Death, which reached Europe in 1348, killing something like a third of the population, meant that for a time the production of any kind of art, including illuminated manuscripts, was very much reduced. At the same time, the influence of the church in affairs of state continued to diminish, so that artists, most of whom had no particular church or monastic connections, now had to turn to royal and noble courts, from Bohemia and

Above: A Pentecost scene by Da Cremona fills this large historiated initital D from a choir book. Italy, c.1490.

Opposite: Resurrection, by Lorenzo Monaco, from an illuminated manu script (Gospels, Bible, Missal) made in Siena. Italy, early 15th century.

Germany to France and the smaller countries of western Europe, for the patrons who would pay for their finest and most costly work.

ILLUMINATED MANUSCRIPTS IN FRANCE

In the mid-fourteenth century, the greatest patrons were to be found in France, surrounding the royal court in Paris. Foremost among them was Jean, Duc de Berri, brother of Charles V of France, himself the possessor of a superb library, and uncle of Charles VI. This latter monarch, so feeble that he

went down in history as Charles the Foolish, created a power vacuum his close relatives lost no time in stepping into, helping themselves to the royal revenues on a lavish scale. Fortunately for posterity, some of their most lavish spending went on books, still very important symbols of wealth and power.

The Duc de Berri not only established a magnificent library, for which he commissioned many gorgeously decorated books with jewel-encrusted covers, including numerous books of hours, psalters and different versions of the *Romance of the Rose*, but also commissioned books as gifts for important occasions, such as royal weddings and birthdays. Since such books were as much about emphasising the power and importance of the Duc de Berri as they were about giving beautiful gifts to others, some of them were virtually priceless and remain some of the most precious relics we have of the medieval period: for instance, the illuminated manuscripts we know as the *Petites Heures du Duc de Berri*, made around 1400, and the *Tres Riches Heures du Duc de Berri*. Both these books

Above: The Parliament of Westminster deposes Richard II and proclaims the Duke of Lancaster Henry IV: a dramatic moment from English history portrayed in *Histoire du Roy d'Angleterre*, Richard II. France, c. 1400.

Opposite: The Ascension: Made in Florence in the age of the Medici. Italy, c.1450.

contain exquisite, jewel-like miniatures by the three celebrated Limbourg brothers.

In the fifteenth century, the French kings, forced out of northern France and Paris by the conquering English (losing the Battle of Agincourt had been the last disaster for Charles VI, who died insane), moved their court to Tours, which now became a centre for court art, including the making of illuminated manuscripts. One of the master illuminators of the period was Jean Fouquet, who, after working for a period in Italy, where he painted a portrait of Pope Eugenius IV, returned to France, bringing the styles and outlook of the Italian

Renaissance with him. He became court painter to Charles VII and Louis XI and both he and his sons are known to have been fine manuscript miniaturists as well as painters.

French-produced illuminated manuscripts of this period were notable for their strong yet delicate colours, into which their illuminators, many of them, like Fouquet, true artists, introduced highlights and shading, and for their expressive faces, and the finely delineated lines and perspectives of their backgrounds. Their influence was felt strongly in surrounding states, including Burgundy, whose cultured dukes included Flanders, with its rich merchant cities, among their lands, and the Netherlands.

Burgundy became a great centre of artistic endeavour in many fields in the fifteenth century, with great artists such as Jan van Eyck having a major influence on the Burgundian style. This style can be seen at its finest in the Flemish *Hastings Hours*, made c.1480, in which superbly painted borders, with wonderful depictions of insects and flowers, frame miniatures of very fine quality.

The *Hastings Hours* is a good example of a noticeable difference between the styles of northern European illuminated manuscripts at this time and those being made in southern Europe, particularly Italy. Northern manuscripts tended to set their miniatures and their borders separately from texts, whereas in Italy, illustrations were still miniatures set in the text area. The northern practice both emphasises the fact that books no longer needed their pictures to explain the text to a largely illiterate audience, and reminds us that book production was already undergoing a revolution: printing from movable type had been going on in Europe for nearly thirty years when the *Hastings Hours* was made. Northern illuminated manuscripts were indicating a way in which printed book design and layout might go.

ILLUMINATED MANUSCRIPTS IN ITALY

Trade and high finance set Italy on the road to the modern world. As the Middle Ages drew to a close, it was the rich merchant cities of northern Italy that provided the foundations on which the Renaissance, that great flowering of the arts and culture, was built. As well as noble rulers established in their courts at Ferrara, Urbino, Milan, Mantua, Naples and other places, Italy had many wealthy merchant families, like the Medici in Florence, round whom centres of art and culture could flourish, and on whose wealth great libraries could be established. Many of these cities – Florence, Bologna, Rome, Milan, Verona, for instance

Above: Sage: from a Renaissance example of the Italian medieval health text book, *Tacuinum sanitatis in medicina*. The Tacuinum was itself based on an earlier Arabic treatise.

Opposite: Proclamation of the renewal of a truce between England and France: European history as told by Jean Froissart in his *Chronicles*. France, early 14th century.

117

Above: A highly stylised rural scene, showing two well-born ladies, catching what appear be hearts floating down from the sky. This from *Emblemes et Devises d'Armour* manuscripts.

— supported the work of several ateliers of illuminators; we can see in them the book publishers of future generations.

The book featured high on the list of any wealthy Italian's important objects. Books could be read in private or studied in learned discussions with groups of friends and scholars. Books, like other forms of art, could also be collected, and the wealthy patrons of the Italian Renaissance were collectors on a grand scale. For books, this meant the establishment of many still famous libraries, where the collections of illuminated manuscripts are stunning indeed. The royal library of Naples, for instance, was augmented by the work of a whole atelier of artists, maintained solely to create and embellish books for it.

Patronage of the arts in Italy long included patronage of book production: one of Giotto's patrons, Cardinal Stefaneschi, also commissioned illuminated manuscripts. Although a grandee of the church, he did not confine his book patronage to religious subjects. Among books known to have been commissioned by him is an impressively large folio book of explanations of a set of laws.

However beautiful their embellishment — and many illuminated manuscripts of the Italian Renaissance were magnificent, indeed — or high the quality their art, Italian manuscripts were different in their layout and design from those of northern Europe. As we have seen, Italian books tended to retain the medieval approach, of integrating text and decoration in a layout that maintained the dominance of the text. There was also, growing out of the Italian Humanist interest in rediscovering the thoughts and philosophies of the Ancient Greeks and Romans, an emphasis on going back to the Antique in design, showing itself in the ivy-leaf and vine stem interlacing, classical vases, garlands and putti that filled borders and frames.

That said, the art of Italian illumination was as finely depicted as that of the north, putting the same emphasis on realism and true perspective that both schools had, in fact, been taught by the early artists of the Italian Renaissance. There was also that same use of contemporary fashion, whether in clothes, hair styles or architecture, that make all the best European illuminated manuscripts such superb sources of social customs and history.

THE LAST DAYS OF THE ILLUMINATED MANUSCRIPT

Although Federigo da Montefeltro, Duke of Urbino, would have nothing to do with printed books in his great library at Urbino, one of the major cultural centres of Europe in his lifetime (he died in 1482), the advent of printing clearly sounded the death knell of the hand-made illuminated manuscript as a major force in the intellectual life of the world.

Above: Bruce of Scotland sends defiance to Edward III of England: a finely detailed picture from a French edition of Jean Froissart's *Chronicles*.

Overleaf: Awetaran in Armenan Illuminated manuscript on vellum written by the scribe Lady Gohar at Germanica in Marash. AD1666.

The scholar Vespasiano, who had helped Federigo collect the books for his library, could write that 'In this library all the books are beautiful in the highest degree, all written with the pen, not one printed, that it might not be disgraced thereby,' but he was swimming against the tide: the demand for books, especially cheaper books, in an increasingly educated world was not to be denied.

It took some time, since until well into the sixteenth century a hand-written illuminated manuscript remained the last word in perfect book production. This was particularly so in Germany, where in the mid-sixteenth century the master illuminator Albert Glockendon and his school produced many

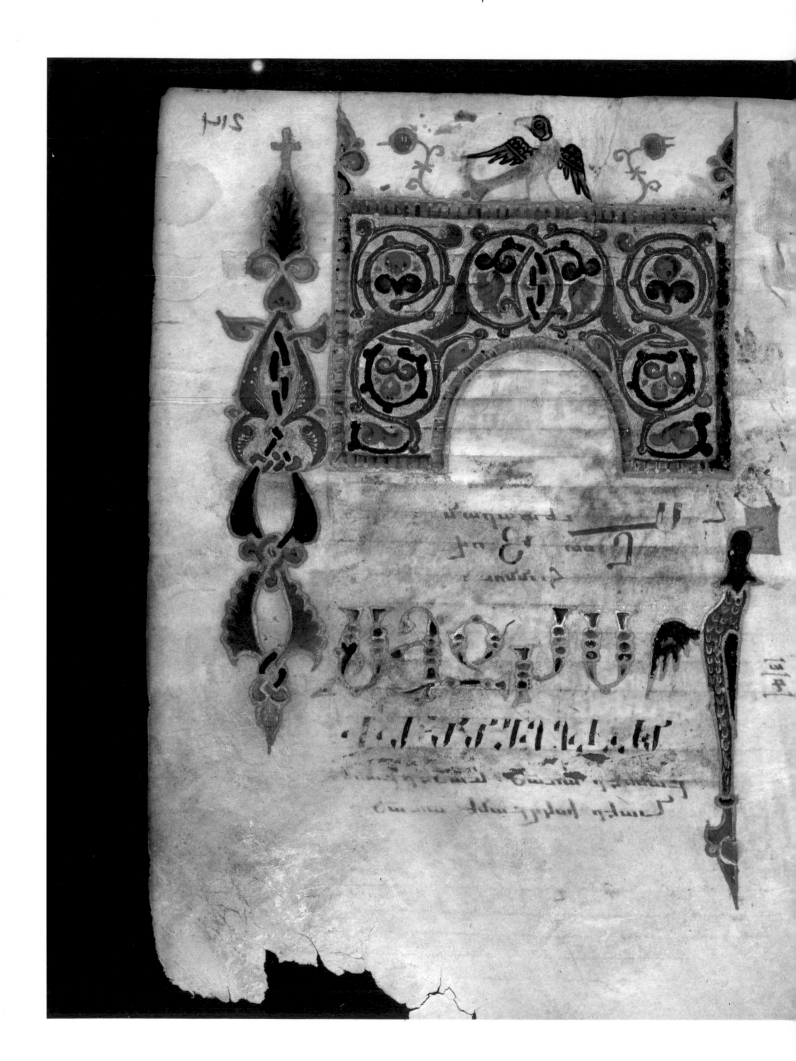

Above: Jean de Wavrin was a celebrated Flemish manuscript artist. This miniature from the *Chronicle of Jan de Wavrin* shows him presenting a copy of his book to King Edward IV.

Opposite: The King of France and the Emperor of Germany in conference: painting from a French edition of Jean Froissart's *Chronicles*.

suberb illuminated manuscripts for royal patrons, such as the *Prayer Book of Albert of Brandenburg*, made in 1524 and the *Prayer Book of William IV of Bavaria*, made in 1535. It was also the practice until well into the century to illustrate by hand and in colour books with printed texts.

But before long, illumination was being reserved for important legal documents such as charters, acts of parliament and the like. In our time, the only glimpses most of us are likely to see of the old art is on Books of Remembrance,

KIII		**Juillet**	
.iij.	g		S̄. thybault
	N.		Saint proces
.xi.	b	N.	Saint apolin
	c	N.	Saint martin
.xix.	d	N.	S̄. dominique
.viij.	e	N.	Octaue. s̄. pierr
	f	N.	S̄. thomas
.xvi.	g	Id.	Saint procope
.v.		Id.	Saint zenon
	b	Id.	Les sept frrrs
.xiij.	c	Id.	Saint benoist
.ij.	d	Id.	Saint list.
	e	Id.	Saint amen
.x.	f	Id.	Saint landri
	g	Id.	Saint bertin

Above: Painting Trades: from a Sienese edition of Pliny the Elder's *Historia Naturalis*. Italy.

Opposite: A Stag Hunt was the chosen image for the month of July in this French manuscript, Tournament in the Water.

listing the dead of past wars, in our churches and cathedrals, or perhaps – if we know a British peer – on the letters patent, written by a Queen's Scribe, that are sent to each new peer of the realm. For the very rich among us, there may still be opportunities for acquiring medieval illuminated manuscripts, as they are not all in libraries and museums. An illuminated *Gospels* made for Henry the Lion sold at auction in 1983 for £8 million, a sign that these wonderful works of art have lost none of their power to obsess us with their beauty and desirability.

That illuminated manuscripts are still sufficiently newsworthy to warrant front page treatment, was recently confirmed by the notice taken of the announcement by an American university, St John's, in Collegeville, Minnesota, that it has commissioned the production of the first new illuminated Bible for 500 years. One of Britain's two Queen's Scribes, plus a team of calligraphers, will be taking six years to complete the commission, writing with goose feather quills on vellum. The work will cost £1.9 million, which would make even that great and splendidly rich patron Lorenzo de Medici swallow hard, while the fact that computers will be doing the page layouts and letter positioning would leave medieval monks, used to pricking and ruling their pages, simply bewildered.

It is satisfying to know, however, that one of the finest art forms of our millennium will find a place of honour in the next.

Index

Page numbers in **boldface** indicate photo captions.

Aachen, palace school at, 47, 51
Aberdeen bestiary, **82**, **93**
Abraham, 87
Adam, **82**
Adelheid of Burgundy, 100
Adoration of the Magi, **51**
Alcuin, 9, 29, 51, 53
Alexander the Great, 15, 111
Alexandria, library at, 30
anatomical man, **95**
Ancient Egyptians, 7, 15
Ancient Greeks, 25, 30, 119
Angelico, Fra, **111**
Anglo-Saxon art, 71, 73
animal skin, 7, 15, 17, 23, 25
Anne of Bohemia, 77, 103
Anne of Brittany, 106
Annunciation, the, 25, **100**
antiphonals, 13
apocalypses, 13
artist, work of the, 35
Arundel Psalter, 77
Ascension, the, **114**
Awetaran in Armenan, **119**

bas de page decorations, 30, 77
Beatus initial, **35**
bees, **93**
Bellville Breviary, 93
Benedictional of St Ethelwold, 73
Berruguete, Pedro, **100**
bestiaries, 13
Bible
    commissioned by Borso d'Este, 106-107
        new illuminated, 125
        stories, 7, 93
        text of, 9, 53, 82
Bible of Saint Andrew of the Woods, **35**
Bibles, 9, 29, **39**, 93
        one-volume, 9, 53
Bibles moralisées, 82, 93
Biblioteca Laurenziana, Florence, **47**
Black Death, 111

Blanche of Castile, **87**
Bohemia, 103, 111
Bohemian style, 77
Book of Durrow, 59, **64**, 67
Book of Hours of Anne of Brittany, **103**
Book of Hours of the Virgin, **103**
Book of Kells, 59, **61**, 64, 67, 69, **71**
Book of Pericopes, 57
Book of Revelations, 13, 79
Book of the Dead, The, 7, **7**, **23**
Books of Hours, 9, **13**, 30, 40, 81, **93**, **95**, **97**, **100**, 106, 113
borders, **23**, 30, 35, **67**, **71**, 73, **77**, **87**, 114
Boucicant Master, **97**
Bourdichon, Jean, **103**
British Library, 53
Bruce of Scotland, **119**
Burgundy, 114
Butler's Lives of the Saints, 59
Byzantine
        art, 39, 51, 57
        influence, **47**
        manuscripts, 67, 71
        style, 40, 57, 59
Byzantium, 30, 37

calandrius bird, **88**
Canon Table, **59**
capitals, 71
Caroline miniscule, 29, 30
Carolingian, 30, 40, 47, 53, 59, 69, 71, 100
Catherine of Valois, 25, **103**
Caxton, William, 77, **79**
Celtic
        art, **23**, 40, 67
        folklore, 61
        Ireland, 59-69
        patterns, 61
        script, 67
Celts, the, 8, 59
Charlemagne, 29, 37, **37**, 39, 40, 47, **47**, 51, 53, 71, 111
Charles III, Emperor, 53
Charles IV, Emperor, 77
Charles V of France, 113
Charles the Bald, King, 95, 100
'Choirs of Angels', **79**

Christianity, 7, 23, 30, 37, 59
Christian Prayers, 79
Chronicles of Jean de Wavrin, **123**
Chroniques de France, 57
churches
        Gothic, 8
        Romanesque, 8
Cicero, Marcus Tullius, **44**
Circle of Pellegrino Di Mariano, 7
Cluny, Abbey, 25, 100
Codex Aurens, 57
codex, 7,15, 17, 25, 30
codices, 8, 23, 30, 37, 39, 40, 53, 59
colours, artists', 30-35, 39, 95
Constantine the Great, **15**, 17, 30, 35
Constantinople, **15**, 30, 37
        effect of, 37-39
Coronation Gospels of the Holy Roman Empire, 51
Count Vivian's Bible (The First Bible of Charles the Bald), 95-100
Crivelli, Taddeo, **106**

Da Crema, **106**
da Montefeltro, Federigo, **100**, 109, 119
damp fold drapery, 73, 87
David, King, **23**, 35, **97**
De arte venani cum avibus, 103
de Hesdin, Jacquemart, **103**
De Senacte, De Amicitis, Paradoxia Stoicorum, **44**
d'Este, Borso, 106
        Bible of, 106
de Wavrin, Jean, **123**
drolleries, 35, **67**, 77, **93**
Duc de Berry, **95**
Durham
        Cathedral, 69
        monastery at, 69, 71
Durrow, monastery at, 59

Eadfrith, Abbot, **30**, 69
Eadwine, **15**, 29
Ecclesia (Psalm 101), **73**
Echternach abbey, 53, 57
Edward III, **119**

Edward IV, **79**, **123**
Eight Circle Cross, **61**
Elizabeth I, **79**
embellishment
        gold, 7, 30, 39, **47**, 57, 67, 69, 73, 95
        red,13
        silver, 7, 39, **47**
Emblemes et Devises d'Armoui, **118**
Emperor of Germany, **123**
English illumination
        first period, 69-71
        post Gothic period, 77
        second period, 71-77
Eumenes II, 15, 17
Evangelistary of Godascalc, 47
evangelists, 67

flight into Egypt, **13**
Florence, 29, 106, 117, 118
Fountain of Life, The, **51**
Fouquet, Jean, 114
Fourth Lateran Council (1215), 81
Frederick I, **82**
Frederick II, 53, **95**, 100
French royal court, 103, 113, 114
Froissart, Jean, **25**
        Chronicles, **25**, **85**, **117**, **119**, **123**
Froissart Manuscripts, 8

genealogy of Christ, **71**, **77**
German Empire, 81
Germany, 53, 100, 111
Gisella, Empress, 57
Glockendon, Albert, 119
Godescalc, 47
Golden Bull of Charles IV, 77
Gorlestch Psalter, **67**
Gorleston Psalter, 73
Gospel lectionary, fragment from, **69**
Gospel of St Matthew, **71**
Gospels, 29, 61, 67, **69**
Gospels, illuminated, 125
Gospels Books (Evangelistary) of Godescalc, **47**, **64**
Gospels of Lothair, 100
Gospels of Saint Médard of

Soissons, **51**
Gothic
    cathedrals, 93
    period, 88
    style, 35, 57, 77, 81, 87, **87**
graduals, 13
Grandes Chroniques, **29**
Gregory the Great, Pope, **37**
Grisaille, **9**
Groot, Gerhard, 103
Gutenberg Bible, 30

Haggandah, **81**
half uncials, 29
Hastings Hours, 114-115
Hebrew illumination, **81**
Hellenistic Byzantine style, 40
Henry I, King, 71
Henry I, Emperor, 53
Henry II, 57
Henry IV, King, **114**
Herodutus, 17
Hildegard, 47, **47**
Histoire du Roy d'Angleterre, **114**
Historia Anglorum, **77**
Historia Naturalis, **17**, **53**, **125**
Hours of Anne of Brittany, 106
Hours of the Cross, **93**
Hours of the Holy Ghost, **93**
Hours of the Virgin, **25**, **93**
human figure, painting the, 87

iconography, Christian, 35
icons, Russian, 39
illuminated, definition of, 7
illumination, definition, of, 30
initials, 25, 35, **39**, 67, 77, **77**
    decorated, 40, 67, 73
    historiated, 30, **88**, **106**, **111**, **113**
    inhabited, 30
    red, 30
insular style, **23**, 40, 47, 59, **61**, **64**, **71**
Iona, 61, 64
Ireland, 59, **59**, 61, 67
Irish monks, 40
Isabella of Bavaria, 103
Italian Renaissance, 111, 117-119

January, **106**
Jarrow, 69
Jean, Duc de Berri, **103**, 106, 113
Jesus (Christ), **13**, **35**, **77**, **88**
July, **97**, **125**
Justinian, Emperor, 39

King of France, **123**

Knights of the Order of the Star, **29**

Lady Gohar, **119**
Lambeth Bible, **77**
lectern, 9, 25
Leo III, Pope, 37
Leo X, **109**
Les Arts Somptuaires, **9**
Life of St Alexis, 77
Limbourg brothers, **97**, 114
Limbourg, Paul, **95**
Lindisfarne, **23**, 61, 69, 71
Lindisfarne Gospels, **23**, 29, **30**, **61**, **64**, 69, 71
liturgical books, 9, 30
lives of the saints, 13
Lothair I, Emperor, 100
Louis IX (St Louis), **87**
Louis XII, **103**
Luttrell Psalter, **23**

MacDurnan Gospels, **71**
Macie Jowski Bible, **44**
Madonna, visitation by, **13**
majuscule uncials, 29
manuscript illumination, origins of, 7-8
Master, Alexis, 77
Master of the Apocrypha Drawings, 73
Master of the Leaping Figures, 73, **73**
Mathilda, Abbess of Quedlinburg, 100
Mathilda, Otto I's mother, 100
May, **97**
Medici, 106, 117
miniatures, 25, 30, 35, 73, 77, **87**, 88, **88**, 93, **93**, 95, **95**, **103**, 109, 114, 117, **123**
Miracles de Notre Dame, **9**
missals, 9, **111**
missionaries, **64**, **67**
Monaco, Lorenzo, **113**
monasteries, 8, 23, 25, 29, 61, 69, 73, 93
Moutier-Granval Bible, 53

National Library of France, Paris, 106
Nativity, the, **106**
Nero, Emperor, **53**
New Testament, 9, 13, **47**
Norman Conquest, 71
Norse invaders, 53
Northumberland, 40, 69

Old Testament, 9, **44**, **61**
oriental influence, 39
Otto I, 53, 57

Otto II, 57, 100
Otto III, 100
Ottonian art, 53-57
Ottonian emperors, 29, 53, 100

Painting Trades, **125**
Palladius, 59
papyrus, 7, 15, 17, **23**
parcheminerie, 25
parchment, 15, 17, 23, 24, 29, 35
Paris, Matthew, 29, 77, **77**
Pentecost, **88**, **113**
Peterborough Psalter, **23**, 77
Petites Heures du Duc de Berri, **113**
Pliny the Elder, 15, **17**, **53**, **125**
Prayer Book of Albert of Brandenburg, 123
Prayer Book of William IV of Bavaria, 123
Prayer Book Master, **30**
Presentation of Christ in the Temple, **47**, **111**
printing
    advent of, **79**, 119
    first printing press, 77
    invention of, 7
Psalter of Ingeborg, **88**
psalters, 9, 13, 30, 77, 81, 95, 113
Pucelle, Jean, 93

Queen Mary Psalter, 88
quill, **15**, **25**, **29**, 125

Raphael, **109**
Registrum, Gregorii, **37**
Resurrection, **113**
Richard II, 77, 103, **114**
roll (*rotuli*) 7, 15, 17
Roman
    alphabet, 29
    Empire, 15, 30, 39
    manuscripts, 71
Romance of the Rose, 113
Romanesque style, 57, 77, 87
Romans, the, 25, 30, 119
Rossi, Franco, **106**
roundels, 39
royal library of Naples, 118

St Albans Abbey, 29, 77, **77**
St Albans Psalter, 77
St Augustine, 9
St Bede, 69
St Benedict, 9
St Columba, 61, 64, 69
St Cuthbert, **23**
St Dominic, **51**
St Ethelwold, 9, 73, 82

St Francis of Assissi, 82, 87, 93
St Gall, monastery at, 69
St Louis Psalter, 87, **87**
St Luke, **47**
St Mark, **23**, **47**
St Matthew, **64**, **67**
St Matthew's Gospel, **13**, **30**
St Patrick, **59**, 61
St Peter, **13**
Sage, **117**
Samson and Delilah, **44**
scribe, work of the, 25-29, 57, 61
scripts, 29-30
scriptorium, **15**, 25, 29, 39, 40, 47, 53, 57, 69, 71, 73, 77, **77**, 95
scrolls, Ancient Egyptian, 7, 17
secular texts, 13
Song of Solomon, 61
S-shape posture of figures, 35, 88, 93
Stag Hunt, **125**
Stefaneschi, Cardinal, 118
Syriac Gospels, 47

Tacuinum sanitatis in medicina, **117**
Theophano, Princess, 57
Tournament in the Water, **125**
Tours, 9, 40, 51, 53, 57, 95, 100, 114
Tree of Jesse, **71**, **77**
Tres Belles Heures, **103**
Tres Riches Heures du Duc de Berri, **97**, **113**
Trinity Apocalypse, **79**

uncial form, 29
universities, 82
Urbino, library at, 119

Vatican Library, 8, 15, 103
vellum, 15, 23, 25, 39, **47**, **88**, **119**, 125
Viking raids, 64, 69
Virgin, the, **40**, **77**
Visconti, Gian Galeazzo, 109
Vulgate Bible, 53
    title page, **111**

Weingarten Chronicles, **82**
Wenzel Bible, 77
Winchester , 9, 73, 82
    style, 73
Winchester Bible, **35**, **61**, 73, **73**

York, 51, 69

Zagba monastery, **47**

PICTURE CREDITS